Through Death's Door

Exploring What Really Happens When We Die

By

Scott Patterson

ISBN: 979-8-9907112-8-0

"Death may be the greatest of all human blessings."
Socrates as recorded by Plato, Apology, 399 BCE

Chapter One

"We found an area of concern and would like to perform additional tests to take a closer look." Most of us will hear these or frighteningly similar words at some point in our lives, spoken softly across a sterile room, beneath the hum of fluorescent lights.

In that instant, time will seem to stand still. Our stomachs will drop, and a cold sweat will break out on our bodies. Our heart rate will increase. A feeling of dread will overwhelm us, and the world will narrow into a single moment of fear.

We'll look at our loved one, their eyes reflecting our own disbelief. A lump may start to form in our throats, and we'll struggle to find our words. *But I'm not ready,* we'll think. *There's still so much to do. So much left undone.*

Death, regardless of its form, is not something we find easy to prepare for. Even those who speak of peace, acceptance, and readiness often find themselves clinging to the fragile thread of life when faced with the reality of letting go.

For many, the idea of death first comes as a whisper. A doctor's concern, a strange pain that lingers, a shadow on a scan. For others, it arrives suddenly, fast, and unexpected, leaving no time for goodbyes.

The truth is, there are countless ways to die beyond just disease, cancer, or illness. Other potentially quicker causes might include unintentional deaths, which encompass injuries, violence, human-related factors, and environmental or miscellaneous causes.

Examples of injuries, accidents, and unintentional deaths include car crashes, falls, drowning, fires and burns, poisoning, drug overdoses, workplace accidents, accidental firearm discharges, natural disasters, and animal attacks.

Violence and human-related causes include suicide, murder/homicide, war/armed conflict, and terrorism. Environmental and miscellaneous causes encompass famine and starvation, extreme weather, air pollution, and toxic exposures.

Yet, by far, the most common cause of death is illness. More than three out of four deaths each year are attributed to disease. The names cancer, heart attack, stroke, Alzheimer's, evoke an almost universal fear. They are whispered in hospital corridors, printed in bold on medical charts, and spoken through tears at kitchen tables around the world.

Diseases can be categorized into two primary forms. Non-communicable diseases and infectious diseases. Non-communicable diseases are the slow, relentless adversaries, characterized by chronic conditions that wear us down over time. They include heart disease, stroke, cancer, chronic lung disease, diabetes, kidney failure, and neurological disorders like Alzheimer's and Parkinson's.

Infectious diseases, by contrast, are ancient predators. They spread from person to person and are transmitted through air, water, or direct contact. They are invisible yet powerful, and they include pneumonia, tuberculosis, HIV/AIDS, malaria, diarrheal infections, and, more recently, COVID-19. They have claimed countless lives across centuries and continents.

Regardless of the path, the destination is the same. Every living being, every human, animal, plant, and even the smallest microbe, is born with one unchangeable truth. We are all born to die. No one escapes. No one leaves this life with their body intact.

So what happens when we die? Science and scientists have studied the physical aspect since the beginning of time. We record the precise time of death as the moment the heart stops beating and all circulatory and cardiac activity ceases. When blood flow stops, it cuts off the oxygen supply to all major organs and tissues.

The brain, the control center of all thought, memory, and consciousness, is the first to be affected. Within three to seven minutes of oxygen deprivation, brain cells begin to die. Consciousness slips away like a fading light. Breathing ceases. Pupils widen and become fixed. The body, once animated by electric impulses, falls into silence.

As the final breath escapes, muscles lose all tone, causing the body to appear limp as it enters a state of flaccidity. The intricate systems that once worked in harmony, including digestion, circulation, and hormonal regulation, cease to function. The integrated dance of the life halt and in its place begins a slow unraveling. From a physiological perspective, this is the beginning of death. But the story of the body doesn't end here. It merely transforms.

Soon after death, the body begins undergoing visible and measurable changes. One of the first is called livor mortis. Livor mortis, also known as postmortem lividity, occurs when blood is no longer pumped by the heart and settles in the lowest parts of the body due to the force of gravity. The skin may develop a purplish-red discoloration in these areas. Livor mortis typically begins within thirty minutes to two hours after death and becomes fixed within six to twelve hours.

The next early change to our bodies after death is rigor mortis, which is the stiffening of the muscles. Following death, calcium ions flood muscle cells, causing sustained contractions that lead to rigidity. Rigor mortis typically begins within two to six hours postmortem.

It starts in the smaller muscles, such as those in the jaw and eyelids, before spreading through the limbs and torso. It reaches its peak at around twelve hours and then, as the tissues begin to break down, it gradually dissipates after twenty-four to forty-eight hours.

After rigor mortis, the body enters decomposition. This is a natural process in which internal enzymes and external microorganisms break down the body, and the body begins to return to the earth from which it originated.

The first stage of decomposition is autolysis, literally self-digestion, which begins as cells break apart from within. In the absence of oxygen, cells begin to rupture, and their contents spill out, releasing enzymes that digest the surrounding tissue. This process typically starts in the liver and pancreas, which are rich in enzymes.

As autolysis progresses, bacteria from the gastrointestinal tract, which are normally harmless to the body, begin to spread throughout the body, accelerating decay. This marks the onset of putrefaction and is characterized by the production of gases such as methane, hydrogen, sulfide, and ammonia. These gases cause the body to bloat and emit a strong, foul odor of decay. The skin may develop greenish or black discoloration, and blisters may form.

The rate and progression of decomposition depend heavily on environmental factors, such as temperature, humidity, exposure to air, and the presence of insects or scavengers. In hot and humid conditions, decomposition occurs more rapidly. In cold or dry environments, the process may be significantly delayed or even paused. Some bodies mummify. Others are preserved in ice or peat bogs for thousands of years.

Human intervention can also change the course of decomposition. Embalming involves injecting preservatives into the body to slow decay, allowing families to hold viewings or ceremonies, or for scientific study. Cremation, on the other hand, accelerates transformation, reducing the body to ash and bone fragments through high-temperature incineration. Burial methods, casket materials, and environmental exposure all influence how, and how quickly, a body returns to the elements.

From a scientific perspective, death is a clear, measurable, and absolute phenomenon. The end of metabolism, the collapse of systems, the silence of cells is a biological event. And yet, for millennia, humanity has believed that there is more to death than just its physiological aspects. We stand beside the lifeless form of someone we love, and though the features remain, we sense that something essential is missing. Something luminous and unseen has departed.

This awareness has given rise to one of the oldest and most profound questions in human history. What happens next? Is death an end, or is it a transition? Is consciousness extinguished, or does it move beyond the body into another realm, another form, another existence? The answers depend on who you ask. Across cultures, across centuries, countless beliefs have been born from this mystery. Each one is an attempt to give meaning to the great unknown.

Every civilization has crafted its own vision of the afterlife, encompassing stories of paradise and punishment, as well as rebirth and release. These beliefs offer comfort, purpose, and structure to the otherwise unbearable idea of nonexistence.

Ancient Egyptians envisioned a journey through the underworld, where their hearts were weighed against a feather to determine their eternal fate. Hindus and Buddhists spoke of reincarnation, where the soul cycles through many lives in pursuit of enlightenment.

Christians envisioned heaven and hell, realms of eternal reward or consequence. Muslims believe in resurrection and judgment before a merciful but just Creator. Indigenous peoples around the world spoke of spirit realms, ancestral lands, and the enduring connection between the living and the dead.

Even modern spiritual movements, from New Age thought to near-death experience research, continue the search for understanding, blending science and mysticism in the quest to explain what happens beyond the final heartbeat.

It is not my intention to teach the doctrines of any particular faith, nor to persuade you toward one belief or another. Instead, I invite you to view these traditions as windows. These are glimpses into how humanity has grappled with mortality through the ages.

Each belief system offers a unique piece of a larger puzzle, a map, perhaps, of a territory none of us has yet returned from to describe with certainty. So let us begin this exploration not with fear, but with curiosity. Let's look together at the stories, symbols, and experiences that have shaped our understanding of death, and in doing so, perhaps uncover what truly lies beyond.

This is our starting point. A place of reference. A threshold. From here, we will explore the worlds of faith, philosophy, and science. And in the spaces between them, examine the truth about what truly happens when we die.

Chapter Two

Since the beginning of time, we've been afraid, curious, and obsessed with death. It must have been puzzling to watch others die and wonder what happened to the friend or family member they knew before death consumed them. Did they go somewhere, or did they disappear from existence entirely?

As far back as four hundred thousand years ago, when **Neanderthals** and **ancient humans** walked our planet, death has been a mystery, an enigma that seemed unsolvable. For a long time, it was believed that Neanderthals and ancient humans were nothing more than mindless beings wandering the earth, discarding the dead without concern or remorse. Then, in the 1930s, a Neanderthal skeleton was found in a shallow pit, suggesting an intentional burial.

During the 1950s and 1960s, several Neanderthal skeletons were found, one of which was buried with pollen from flowers. This discovery led to the idea that Neanderthals might have had symbolic burials, and implied they possibly held spiritual beliefs or even practiced some form of religion.

Many experts disputed the reported burials and the presence of pollen, arguing that insects likely carried the pollen to the site. They maintained that their own interpretations were correct and that the findings must have alternative explanations.

In the 2000s, recent excavations and dating techniques provided strong support for the theory that Neanderthals buried their dead. There has also been evidence of communal care, where some individuals lived a long time after a debilitating injury. This communal care suggests social bonds and possibly a view that life and death are closely connected.

Although there is no direct evidence that Neanderthals had a structured religion, symbolic behaviors such as body decoration, grave placement, cave art, and communal care suggest they engaged in abstract thinking, possibly including beliefs about death and the afterlife.

If Neanderthals were contemplating the afterlife and their creator, they must have been in shock when they encountered anatomically modern humans, or what we now refer to as Homo sapiens, in Europe and Asia approximately forty thousand to sixty thousand years ago.

As our ancestors evolved, and Neanderthals gradually became extinct, burials became increasingly elaborate and clearly symbolic. Graves began to be adorned with symbolic pigments. Figurines that could be connected to fertility, life cycles, or spirits, as well as decorative items such as beads, tools, animal bones, cave paintings, carvings, and totem-like arrangements, may have marked the beginning of ancestor worship. All of these behaviors seemed to reflect a growing concern with life after death, the spirit world, or ritual mourning.

While it's impossible to know their exact beliefs, both Neanderthals and early humans exhibited behaviors that suggest an awareness of mortality, respect for the dead, and possibly a belief in something beyond this life or existence. These practices will lay the foundational groundwork for the religions and spiritual belief systems that will emerge in later civilizations.

Around the same time Neanderthals and early Homo sapiens were encountering each other in Europe and Asia, the ancestors of **Aboriginal Australians** were developing the rich spiritual traditions known today as the Dreaming. Aboriginal Australians are the oldest continuous culture on Earth, with archaeological evidence dating back at least fifty thousand to sixty-five thousand years. Dreamtime beliefs are also the longest spiritual traditions in the world.

In Aboriginal spirituality, the "Dreaming" (or "Dreamtime") refers to a timeless, spiritual domain outside of linear history, in which ancestral beings created the land, animals, people, and customs. These ancestral spirits are ever-present and continue to influence the physical world. Dreaming is not a past event but a continuous, living reality.

When an Aboriginal person dies, their spirit is believed to return to the Dreaming. Death is viewed as part of the cyclical flow of life, encompassing birth, life, death, and rebirth into the land and spirit world. Some groups believe that the soul travels to a specific spiritual site or re-enters the land, waters, or sky to be reborn again in some form. Others maintain that the spirit remains in its sacred homeland, where it joins the ancestors and continues to exist as part of the community's spiritual ecosystem.

The **Bushmen of Africa,** also known as the San, are another of the oldest known continuous cultures on Earth. The San probably inhabited Africa as much as forty thousand years ago in modern-day Botswana, Namibia, South Africa, and Angola. Although rock art has been discovered across southern Africa, dating back approximately twenty-seven thousand years and depicting spiritual and shamanistic themes, other archaeological evidence suggests that the San's spiritual beliefs date back to around 10,000 BCE.

The San see death as a transition. They believe it's not an end but a return to the spirit world or cosmic order. The soul, or spiritual essence, is believed to depart from the body and journey to the spirit realm. Sometimes it would remain to influence the living. They believed that death was rarely natural and that sorcery, broken taboos, or spiritual imbalance were the deeper causes.

Ancestors played a powerful role in their beliefs about death. Some believed the spirits of the dead could linger and that they might bring either blessings or misfortune. Because of this, they treated the dead with respect to avoid angering the spirits.

The San religion isn't organized like modern religions with a founder or a written doctrine. Instead, it's deeply rooted in animistic and shamanistic traditions, based on the belief in a supreme creator often portrayed as a trickster. Animism is the belief that objects, places, and creatures possess a distinct spiritual essence or soul. The San also believed in the presence of lesser spirits associated with animals, ancestors, and the natural world.

It's believed that **indigenous North Americans** arrived between fifteen thousand and twenty thousand years ago. Archaeological findings, oral tradition, and historical records indicate they developed their beliefs about death and dying around 10,000 BCE. Indigenous North American cultures are incredibly diverse, encompassing hundreds of distinct nations, each with its own languages, oral histories, and spiritual frameworks.

Despite this diversity, many Indigenous peoples share core beliefs about the soul, death, the afterlife, and the sacred interconnectedness of all living things. These traditions were usually not written down but were passed down through generations using stories, ceremonies, rituals, and symbols.

Most Indigenous groups believed in a soul or spirit that continues to exist after physical death. Often, this soul was perceived as complex or as possessing multiple aspects. While interpretations vary, many traditions involve a spiritual realm that often mirrors the natural world, where the soul finds peace, guidance, or transformation.

The **Iroquois** believed that if rites were performed correctly, the souls would journey to the west to a land of the dead, where harmony would continue. The **Cherokee** believed that the afterlife was seen as another world closely connected to this one, maintaining harmony if the person lived in accordance with sacred balance. The **Hopi** believed in a cyclical journey between this world and the underworld, where souls became part of a continued cycle of renewal.

Approximately seven thousand years after indigenous North Americans developed their beliefs about death and dying, the Mesopotamian and Egyptian civilizations began to develop their own distinct religions. Although both of these societies were polytheistic in nature, their view on death and the afterlife were vastly different.

In 3000 BCE, the ancient **Egyptians** had some of the most elaborate and well-documented beliefs and rituals concerning death and the afterlife in human history. Their entire religious and cultural system placed immense importance on the concept of life after death, and many of their greatest achievements, such as the pyramids, were directly tied to preparing for that afterlife.

The Egyptians believed that the afterlife held a paradise, but the dead had to pass spiritual tests and be judged worthy of entering the paradise. They also believed that souls would be judged and weighed against the feather of Ma'at by the god Anubis. If the heart was heavier than the feather due to sin or untruth, it was devoured by Ammit, a monstrous hybrid creature, and the soul would cease to exist, resulting in true death.,

The **Mesopotamian** beliefs about death and dying were deeply shaped by their worldview. Uncertainty, powerful gods, and an emphasis on living life fully characterized it, as the afterlife was viewed as a shadowy and grim place rather than a reward.

Their underworld was for everyone. Kings, peasants, heroes, and villains. It was a dim, joyless realm, often described as a dusty, cavernous, subterranean world. There was no judgment, no paradise, no punishment. Just eternal grayness that couldn't be escaped.

The **Indus Valley Civilization**, also known as the Harappan Civilization, lived in the modern-day Pakistan and Northwestern

India area between 2600 and 1900 BCE. They left no known written texts that can be definitively translated, which makes their beliefs on death and dying speculative.

Burying the body was the most common practice for the Indus Valley. The careful placement of the body may indicate ritual or symbolic meaning. Adding pottery, beads, bangles, tools, and small figurines to the grave suggests a belief in some kind of afterlife or, at the very least, a concern for the comfort and status of the dead.

Of course, all of this is speculative, and some experts have suggested that the Vedic concept of afterlife and ritual cremation may have evolved from or alongside earlier Harappan practices. Some believe that proto-Shiva-like figures, such as the Pashupati seal, suggest early forms of religious iconography, derived from the Greek word "graphos," meaning "to write or draw," which later developed into the iconography seen in Hinduism.

The **Canaanites** were a group of ancient Semitic-speaking people who lived in the Levant from the 2nd millennium BCE. The Levant encompassed modern-day Israel, Palestine, Lebanon, western Jordan, and western Syria. They had a rich and complex belief system that included distinctive views on death, dying, and the afterlife.

To the Canaanites, death was a dark, unwelcome realm. They believed the dead went to an underworld called Mot, which was ruled by the god of death, Mot. His name literally means death. This underworld was gloomy, dusty, and silent. The dead were cut off from joy, food, and divine favor. There was no reward or punishment, but the afterlife was seen as a bleak, shadowy existence.

There was no clear understanding of resurrection or moral judgment after death, and the Canaanite focus was on life and the continuation of one's legacy rather than a hopeful afterlife. To the Canaanites, ancestors were believed to retain power or influence and would be honored, fed, or appeased. Neglecting the dead could bring misfortune to the surviving family.

Judaism's patriarchal period begins with Abraham, who is believed to have lived around 2000-1800 BCE in Mesopotamia. The formal emergence is often dated to roughly 1200-1000 BCE, when Moses received the Ten Commandments and the Torah at Mount Sinai. Some argue that the entire Torah was given to Moses on Mount Sinai, while others claim it was revealed to him over the course of forty years in the wilderness.

Judaism approaches death with seriousness, humility, and deep respect. It's based on the belief that life is sacred and death is a transition, not an end. Judaism holds that the soul is eternal and returns to God after death.

This spiritual afterlife is where the soul finds rest, either in a paradise or in union with God. Some Jewish traditions, especially those of the Orthodox faith, believe in a future bodily resurrection during the Messianic Age. Others believe in a type of judgment or purification process, though the concept of hell is not central.

In approximately 1500 BCE, three civilizations began to develop spiritual beliefs. The **Polynesian religions,** the **Mesoamerican religions,** and **Hinduism** all started to form. Mesoamerican religions, including the Olmec, Maya, and Aztecs, emerged in the west, while Hinduism originated in the east, and Polynesian religions developed in the central and southern Pacific Ocean.

In Mesoamerican cultures, the Maya and Aztec civilizations saw death not as the end of life, but as a powerful transformation that begins a journey into the spiritual realms. Both the Maya and the Aztecs viewed the universe as multi-layered, filled with divine beings and a cyclical nature. Death was a gateway to transformation, not a final destination. Interestingly, it was the Mayans who first had a resurrection story.

The **Maya** believed the cosmos consisted of thirteen upper worlds and nine underworlds, with the human realm situated at its center. Death often led the soul to Xibalba, the Maya underworld, ruled by gods of disease and death.

As Mesoamerican cultures established their beliefs in the west, **Hinduism** was developing in the east during the period known as the Proto-Vedic Period. The Vedic religion is the oldest major religion still in existence, which encompasses karma, dharma, reincarnation, and a broad pantheon of gods.

Polynesia is often described as a triangle with Hawaii, New Zealand, and Easter Island forming its corners. Polynesian and Hawaiian beliefs about death are deeply rooted in the idea that everything, including people, animals, plants, rocks, rivers, mountains, trees, and even the wind and stars, are spiritually alive and interconnected.

This is also known as animism and is strongly based on the importance of ancestors and the idea of spiritual and sacred restrictions. Death is seen as a transition, and communities perform rituals to guide the spirit, cleanse the living, and preserve harmony.

In **Polynesian** beliefs, souls are considered physical entities that often depart through the tear duct and journey to the Polynesian spirit world or ancestral homeland, known as Pulotu. Some spirits may linger among family, and proper rituals determine whether they stay as protectors or dissipate.

Some of the dangers in the underworld included deities like Māori Whiro, who fed on bodies to gain power. Because of this belief, people practiced cremation to prevent spiritual harm.

Hawaiians believed that ancestor spirits would sometimes reside in volcanoes, oceans, or plains, depending on a person's spiritual life. The bones would hold a person's spiritual power and needed special handling. They would be removed, cleaned, wrapped, and either interred or buried in hidden or sacred places.

Hinduism emerged from the Proto-Vedic period or the early stage of Vedic culture. In Hinduism, death is not an end but a transition, a passage from one stage of existence to another. Central to this worldview are the beliefs in Samsara, the cycle of birth, death, and rebirth, and karma, the moral law of cause and effect. It is viewed as a natural part of life, with the focus on the soul's journey rather than attachment to material possessions.

Hindus believe the soul is eternal, and the body is temporary. It is seen as clothes the soul wears and discards. After death, the soul leaves the body and is reborn into another form of life. This life form could be human, animal, or divine. The life form received as well as one's next life is determined by the actions and intentions of their life, also called Karma. The ultimate goal is to escape the cycle of birth and death, achieving liberation and union with ultimate reality.

Chapter Three

Around 1200-1000 BCE, one of the earliest monotheistic religions emerged. It was called **Zoroastrianism** and was named after its prophet Zoroaster. It was practiced in Iran and possibly southwestern Afghanistan. It had a unique and detailed belief system regarding death, the afterlife, and rituals for the dead. It focused on the ongoing cosmic battle between good and evil, and taught that a person's choices in life determined their fate in the afterlife.

Approximately three hundred years later, around 1200 BCE, the linguistic and cultural ancestors of the **Celts** began to emerge, sharing mythologies and animistic beliefs. The Celts were a diverse group of tribal peoples who lived across Europe, prominently in what is now Ireland, Scotland, Wales, France, and parts of Central Europe.

They held rich and layered beliefs about death and the afterlife. Much of what we know comes from archaeology, Roman accounts, and later medieval Irish and Welsh literature, which preserved echoes of pre-Christian Celtic religion.

The Celts saw death as a passage to another realm, not a final departure. Their worldview was cyclical, with life, death, and rebirth forming an eternal rhythm. They believed the soul survived death and continued its journey in another world, often described as the Otherworld. Some traditions held that the soul might reincarnate, returning in a new body.

The otherworldly realm was known by different names and was described as a paradise filled with youth, beauty, abundance, and peace. Greek and Roman writers, such as Julius Caesar, noted that the Druids, the Celtic priestly class, believed in the transmigration of souls. "They believe that souls do not perish, but pass after death from one body to another..."–Julius Caesar, Gallic War

Archaeologists believe that the **Greeks and Romans** started around 1000 BCE, with the Homeric texts contributing to their stories in 500 CE. They were polytheistic societies that believed in many gods. They held rich, symbolic, and sometimes fearful beliefs about death and the afterlife, which were deeply embedded in their mythology, philosophy, and rituals. Although each culture had its own traits, Roman beliefs were heavily influenced by earlier Greek ideas.

The **Greeks** believed that death marked the departure of the soul from the body. The soul journeyed to the underworld, which was ruled by Hades. To the Greeks, the afterlife wasn't heaven or hell. It was a shadowy realm where souls lived.

The **Romans** also believed that the soul journeyed to the Underworld. They also believed in ancestral spirits that were believed to protect the family if they were properly appeased during burial, as well as in death. This does not mean that the Greeks did not believe in reincarnation.

In the 6th century BCE, Pythagoras believed in metempsychosis. That is the transmigration of the soul into different bodies, including animals. Between 427 and 347 BCE, Plato's works, such as the Phaedrus and Phaedo, describe a cycle of rebirth, where the soul passes through multiple lives in pursuit of purification and wisdom. He believed the soul remembers knowledge from previous lives. This concept is known as anamnesis, or the act of recollection.

Most Romans did not believe in reincarnation. Their focus was on the soul going to the Underworld or being honored as an ancestor spirit. However, some Roman philosophers and mystics who were influenced by Greek ideas accepted the possibility of reincarnation.

According to archaeologists, many other cultures started their spiritual beliefs around the same time as the Greeks and Romans, about 1000 BCE. Although China has over five thousand years of history, archaeologists say that Chinese folk religion began during this period, along with the Yoruba religion, the Sámi Shamanism, and the Zulu and Southern African tribes.

Chinese folk religion is a broad and ancient system of spiritual beliefs, practices, and customs. They view death as a passage into another realm rather than as an end. In its present form, it blends elements from ancestor worship, Taoism, Confucianism, Buddhism, and ancient animistic traditions. It has guided Chinese attitudes toward the afterlife for thousands of years.

They believe that every person has two souls. The yin soul, which stays with the body and may linger at the gravesite, and the yang soul, which is more ethereal and ascends to the heavens. Harmony between the souls is seen as key during life, and managing them after death ensures a peaceful afterlife.

After death, the soul passes into the spirit world, which may involve a period of judgment and punishment for one's earthly deeds. It also believes in reincarnation through the wheel of life, a belief shared with Chinese Buddhism.

If ancestors are honored properly, the deceased becomes a benevolent ancestor spirit, protecting descendants. If neglected, the spirit could become angry, transforming into a wandering or hungry ghost and bringing misfortune.

The **Yoruba** people are primarily found in Nigeria, Benin, and Togo. They have a rich and deeply spiritual worldview, including complex beliefs about death and the afterlife. Their understanding blends ancestor veneration, spirit cosmology, and ritual continuity. It remains influential today. Not only in West Africa but also throughout the global communities of people of African descent who were dispersed from their ancestral homelands in Africa.

They believe in the visible world, or the physical realm, where the living reside. They also believe in an invisible, spiritual world, where deities, ancestors, and spirits dwell. When a person dies, their soul leaves the visible world and transitions to the invisible, spiritual world. This is not necessarily seen as an end but as a passage to another phase or existence.

Each person is made up of spiritual components. At the center of this is the spiritual head or personal destiny. It plays a key role in a person's fate. The life force, or breath, returns to the unseen spiritual world after death. Each person also has a creator or personal deity, as well as a higher self that exists in the invisible spirit realm. The way someone lives, their moral quality, and their choices help determine what happens after death.

If a person has lived a morally upright life, had children, and been properly buried, they may become an ancestor or respected spirit who continues to influence and protect their descendants. They might also be reincarnated, usually within their family line. A newborn may carry the spirit or traits of a recently departed relative, especially if named after them. This is seen as a spiritual return, not just a biological continuation.

Sámi shamanism is the traditional spiritual practice of the Sámi people, who are Indigenous to northern Norway, Sweden, Finland, and the Kola Peninsula of Russia. They have a rich belief system centered around death and the afterlife. While beliefs varied slightly by region and clan, some common ideas included the belief that the soul is multifaceted.

The Sámi believed a person possesses multiple souls. The free soul could travel in dreams or during trance states. The body needed to keep itself alive, so the guardian spirit protected each individual. When a person dies, their soul separates, and their destination depends on how they lived and the proper rituals they performed.

The Sámi believed in a continuation of life after death in the land of the dead. This world mirrored the living world and was sometimes imagined to be located beneath a lake, a mountain, or under the earth. In this spirit realm, the dead continued to live similarly to how they had lived in life, pursuing their previous occupations, such as hunting and herding.

It was not seen as a place of judgment, like heaven or hell, but a place of return to the ancestors. Ancestor spirits could influence the living, for better or worse, so honoring and appeasing them was essential for protection, fertility, and good fortune.

The **Zulu** and other **Southern African** traditional belief systems, such as the Xhosa, Sotho, Tswana, and Ndebele peoples, hold deeply rooted spiritual beliefs about death, the afterlife, and ancestral connections. These beliefs are influenced by African cosmology, which emphasizes harmony among the living, the ancestors, nature, and the divine.

Death was not seen as an end, but as a transformation into the realm of ancestors. The dead would join the ancestors, where they would watch over the family. Ancestors were revered, not worshiped like gods, and they played a crucial role in guidance, protection, fertility, health, and success.

To become an ancestor, one must have lived a good, moral life and received the proper burial rituals. The spirit was believed to continue to exist after death in a parallel, unseen world. The dead were believed to remain close to the family. They are ever-present and must be respected and honored.

The belief in reincarnation throughout history appears to have been shaped by the warring times in which people lived. Believing in another life after this one helped shape one's beliefs about the importance of life and made it easier to die for a cause.

If there were different levels of afterlives for different types of death, and dying in battle was the top rung, many young men would gladly give their lives in battle to achieve that level of paradise in the afterlife.

Chapter Four

Atheism, as we understand it, is relatively new in our existence. In modern times, being an atheist means you don't believe in God and therefore don't believe in an afterlife. At death, the lights go out, and that is all there is. However, if you ever speak to an ambulance driver or a medic, they will tell you that everyone goes out praying and that there is no such thing as an atheist.

Believing there is no god and therefore no afterlife is the modern-day understanding of atheism. It is not how ancient people viewed it. The word "atheist" comes from the Greek *"a-theos,"* meaning "without gods." Originally, it was used as a slur to accuse people of impiety or heresy, not as something they would choose for themselves. In the modern sense, a person who doesn't believe in any gods is an atheist, and this belief became clearer during the Age of Enlightenment in the 17th and 18th centuries.

This isn't to say that our prehistoric ancestors didn't have questions about whether God existed, but written and archaeological evidence for the word "atheist" appeared around 500 BCE, when Protagoras was quoted as saying, "About the gods, I cannot say whether they exist or not..."

Democritus proposed a materialist universe made only of atoms and void, with no need for gods. Epicurus believed gods might exist, but they were uninterested in human affairs. This implied there was no afterlife.

Pythagoras and Plato were deeply spiritual but challenged the popular mythology of the gods. However, the most famous "atheist" of the time was Socrates. Socrates was accused of impiety and brought to trial in Athens.

The formal charges included impiety or "not acknowledging the gods whom the city acknowledges and introducing new divinities." The accusation also claimed he was corrupting the youth by influencing young men such as Plato, Alcibiades, and others through his questioning of authority and traditional beliefs.

Socrates denied being an atheist. He claimed to believe in a divine moral order and often referred to a divine voice or Daimonion, which could be interpreted as a guiding spirit or inner voice.

However, he did challenge traditional beliefs about the Olympian gods and encouraged critical thinking. Critical thinking has alarmed conservative leadership throughout the ages, and the fear of critical thinking has caused millions of deaths. Socrates was found guilty by a narrow vote. He was sentenced to death and was executed by drinking hemlock shortly after the trial.

The 5th century BCE also marks the beginning of our modern religions that we know today. Buddhism, Jainism, and Confucianism had their beginnings, with Taoism appearing in the 4th century BCE.

Siddhartha Gautama, who became known as the Buddha, founded **Buddhism**. Siddhartha Gautama was born a prince in ancient India around the 6th century BCE. He was raised in luxury and carefully shielded from suffering by his father, King Śuddhodana.

A sage had warned his father that his son would either become a great ruler or a spiritual teacher. To ensure Siddhartha chose the path of kingship, the king kept him confined within the palace, surrounded by beauty, pleasure, and youth, and forbade any exposure to illness, aging, or death.

Despite these efforts, Siddhartha eventually ventured beyond the palace walls and encountered the "Four Sights" that were foretold by the sage. The "Four sights" included an old man, a sick person, a corpse, and a wandering ascetic. These revelations deeply disturbed Siddhartha and awakened his desire to understand and transcend human suffering.

He left behind his royal life, wife, and child to become a wandering seeker, and after years of meditation and ascetic practice, he attained enlightenment beneath the Bodhi tree. Realizing the Four Noble Truths and the path to liberation, he became the Buddha, "the Enlightened One," and spent the rest of his life teaching others how to overcome suffering through wisdom and compassion.

Buddhism teaches that life is part of a continuous cycle of birth, death, and rebirth, and that the form of one's next rebirth depends on karma. The moral consequences of one's actions. The ultimate goal is nirvana, which is a release from this cycle. Nirvana is not considered heaven but a state beyond suffering, craving, and ego. An enlightened being or a Buddha does not take rebirth after death.

Jainism is one of the oldest religions in India, dating back to around the 6th century BCE. It holds a deeply spiritual and ascetic view of death, shaped by its core values of non-violence, karma, soul liberation, and self-discipline. For Jains, death is a transition, not an end. It's an opportunity for the soul to move closer to soul liberation, or complete liberation from the cycle of birth, death, and rebirth.

Jainism teaches that every living being possesses an eternal, conscious soul. The soul is bound by karma, a subtle matter that adheres to it due to one's actions, emotions, and thoughts. Death is the release of the soul from the body, but it does not mean complete liberation from the cycle of birth, death, and rebirth unless one is spiritually pure.

The form of the next rebirth can be a human, an animal, a plant, a hell being, or a celestial being. The form an individual takes depends on the karmic weight of their actions. Good karma results in better rebirths, while negative karma leads to lower forms of existence. The soul's liberation occurs when all karma is shed. Once liberated, the soul rises to the top of the universe and exists in a state of eternal bliss and consciousness, no longer subject to birth or death.

Confucianism, rooted in the teachings of Confucius (Kong Fuzi, 551–479 BCE), is more a philosophy of ethical living and social harmony than a religion concerned with the afterlife. However, it has had a profound influence on Chinese attitudes toward death, ancestor worship, and ritual, shaping funeral customs for centuries.

Confucians believe that death is a part of life. Confucius emphasized moral duty in this life, not speculation about what happens after death. Analects 11:12 states, "You do not understand even life. How can you understand death?" Confucius emphasized the importance of being a virtuous person in the present, rather than preparing for heaven or rebirth.

Although he didn't specify an afterlife, he strongly emphasized ancestral reverence. Ancestors were believed to have a continuing presence and influence over the living. He also recognized heaven as a moral force but avoided theological specifics. Death might result in joining ancestral spirits or becoming a revered ancestor, but there is no fixed view of heaven or hell.

Taoism is part of a philosophical and religious tradition that originated in ancient China and has evolved over two thousand five hundred years. The foundational text, the Tao Te Ching, is attributed to Lao Tzu. It was likely written between 600 and 400 BCE. Taoist and Daoist beliefs about death and dying are deeply rooted in the philosophy of balance, natural flow, and immortality.

Unlike religions that focus on judgment or final destinations, Taoism emphasizes harmony with the eternal, mysterious force that flows through all life. Taoists view death as a natural part of the cycle of life, not as something to be feared. Death is not an end but a return to the Tao, the universal source.

Taoists also believed that the soul consists of the yin and the yang, and the goal was to maintain harmony between these forces in life and guide them properly in death. Early Taoism doesn't describe heaven or hell in the same way as Abrahamic religions do. Instead, the soul may dissolve into the Tao or continue in another form. Later, popular or religious Taoism incorporated ideas of spirit realms, celestial bureaucracy, and multiple heavens and hells. This was influenced by Buddhism and folk beliefs.

All of these early religions originated before the Common Era and can be grouped into broad categories based on their views of the afterlife.

The first group includes Hinduism, Buddhism, Jainism, Taoism, Chinese Folk Religion, Sámi traditions, Aboriginal beliefs, Indigenous North American spirituality, the Yoruba religion, and Polynesian faiths. These systems share a belief in reincarnation, or the idea that the soul returns to the earthly realm after death, taking a new form as a human, animal, or other living being.

The second group, comprising Mesopotamian, Greek, Roman, Canaanite, Celtic, Sámi, and San traditions, envisioned a gray underworld, a shadowy realm where souls wandered endlessly with no escape. Existence there was often portrayed as joyless and eternal, a kind of limbo rather than punishment or paradise.

The third group includes faiths that envisioned a promised land or paradise after death. Zoroastrianism, the later texts of Judaism, the Egyptian religion, Yoruba, Zulu, Polynesian, and Chinese folk faiths all described a destination where souls could live in peace, luxury, or reunion with their ancestors. Their reward for a life well lived.

Other traditions took different paths entirely. Early Buddhism taught that the ultimate goal was nirvana. Not a physical place, but the cessation of desire, suffering, and rebirth. Upon achieving enlightenment, a being is freed from the cycle of existence and enters a state often described as transcendent nothingness or complete liberation.

Jainism shares similarities with Buddhism but views liberation differently. The goal is not freedom from rebirth itself but the soul's ascent to a state of perfect stillness and detachment at the top of the universe. This is not "nothingness," but rather an eternal, motionless existence beyond change and worldly involvement.

Confucianism, meanwhile, largely avoids speculation about the afterlife. It focuses instead on moral conduct, social harmony, and duty to family and society. While ancestor veneration is central, there is no fixed doctrine about what happens after death. Some Confucians believe the soul disperses into nature, while others consider the question unknowable. The prevailing mindset can be summed up as: Live well now, honor your ancestors, and let the afterlife take care of itself.

Finally, Greek philosophy, especially that of the Epicureans, held that death is the end—no soul, no afterlife, only the cessation of existence. Likewise, the Canaanite and Mesopotamian views of a bleak underworld bordered on nihilism. It describes an eternity devoid of joy, hope, or meaning, with a mere shadowy existence without renewal.

Chapter Five

Christianity originated in the 1st century AD in Judea, the southern region of ancient Israel. Jesus was crucified during the rule of the Roman governor Pontius Pilate. Shortly after Jesus' death, his followers began spreading his teachings, claiming he had risen from the dead. This marked the beginning of the Christian movement, originally seen as a Jewish sect.

Christian beliefs about death and dying center on the hope of eternal life, the resurrection of the body, and the soul's union with God. These beliefs are rooted in the teachings of Jesus Christ, whose death and resurrection are seen as the ultimate triumph over death.

Death is a transition from earthly life to eternal life. The soul continues to exist and faces judgment, either going to heaven, hell, or purgatory. Based on Jesus' resurrection, Christians believe the dead will one day be raised bodily at the end of time, also known as the last judgment. This belief is found in both the Apostolic and Nicene Creeds, which are central to most Christian denominations.

Heaven is viewed as an everlasting union with God, characterized by joy, peace, and the absence of suffering. Hell is seen as a separation from God, associated with suffering or regret. Purgatory is primarily a Catholic belief and is considered a temporary state of purification before entering heaven. Entry into eternal life depends on one's faith in Jesus Christ, repentance of sins, and God's grace. Good deeds and living a moral life demonstrate faith in Jesus Christ.

Ethiopian Orthodox Christianity is one of the world's oldest Christian traditions. It was established in Ethiopia around 330 CE, and holds deep and unique beliefs about death and the afterlife that blend early Christian theology with ancient Jewish influences, local African customs, and monastic spirituality. These beliefs are reflected in both doctrine and rich ritual practices, often differing in tone and detail from Western Christianity.

Ethiopian Orthodox Christians believe that death is not an end but the soul's departure from the body to face judgment. The soul immediately enters a transitional phase where it is escorted by angels to be judged by God. Emphasis is placed on living a righteous life filled with prayer, fasting, confession, and humility to prepare for death.

A central belief of Ethiopian Orthodox Christians is that the soul journeys for forty days after death before reaching its final destination. During the first three days, the soul stays near the body and home. From day four to day forty, the soul is guided by angels through various spiritual realms, and on day forty, the soul appears before God's throne for a preliminary judgment. This is not the final judgment, but determines the soul's condition until the final resurrection.

If the soul is deemed righteous, it is taken to heaven where it rejoices in the presence of God, the angels, and saints. Hell is for the unrepentant, a place of separation from God filled with anguish and regret. The final judgment will take place at the Second Coming of Christ, when all souls will be reunited with their bodies and judged eternally.

While not called "Purgatory," there is a strong belief in intercessory prayer, almsgiving, and masses offered for the souls of the dead to alleviate their suffering and aid them in entering paradise. The living have a duty to assist the dead through spiritual works.

Ethiopian Orthodox Christianity honors death with reverence, community support, and spiritual duty. The rituals aim to assist the soul, comfort the grief-stricken, and preserve the connection between the living and the dead within God's eternal plan. Their distinctive mix of ancient Christian beliefs, Jewish customs, and African spirituality makes this tradition one of the most captivating in Christendom.

Islam was established in the 7th century CE in the Arabian Peninsula, specifically in the city of Mecca, which is now located in Saudi Arabia. The Prophet Muhammad started receiving revelations from Allah through the angel Gabriel. These revelations were eventually compiled into the Qur'an, the holy book of Islam. Islam means "submission" (to the will of God), and the act of breathing life into Adam symbolizes God's direct involvement in giving each human their soul.

Islam believes that death is a transition and not an end. The Qur'an teaches that life is a test, and how one lives determines their fate after death. The soul is eternal and leaves the body at death. There is no reincarnation. Each person has one life, followed by resurrection and judgment.

The soul departs the body and enters a different realm. At death, a person's soul separates and enters a state called Barzakh, which serves as a waiting period until the day of judgment. On that day, Allah will resurrect all people, judge them, and send the righteous to a place of eternal peace and joy. The wicked will be sent to a place of suffering and punishment.

Shinto is Japan's native religion. It was a collection of traditional Japanese spiritual practices passed down orally through generations before the Japanese government started to write and organize Shinto beliefs and rituals. This was partly to unify the country under an imperial ideology. This occurred in the 7th century CE.

In Shinto, death is viewed as a natural but spiritually impure event. While Shinto emphasizes life, vitality, and harmony with nature, it also holds complex, respectful views about death and the spirit world, often in conjunction with Japanese Buddhist practices. Shinto's approach to death centers on maintaining harmony with ancestral spirits and the natural world, and ensuring proper rituals are done to avoid spiritual disorder or impurity.

Death is regarded as a ritual impurity. It isn't evil, but it disturbs the harmony that Shinto values. Therefore, funerals and death rituals are usually conducted outside of Shinto Shrines, which are places of purity and life. After death, a person's soul becomes a spirit that remains in the human realm. If properly treated with rituals, the "reikon," soul or life energy, eventually transforms into a protective ancestor spirit. If neglected, the soul may become a restless, wandering spirit, often depicted in ghost stories.

Traditional Shinto does not describe a specific afterlife but rather a vague otherworld ruled by Izanami, the goddess of death. Yomi is not a place of judgment but a shadowy realm where the dead dwell. With Buddhist influence, many Japanese today also believe in reincarnation, karma, or the Pure Land.

The **Norse peoples,** Vikings, and other Germanic tribes of Scandinavia had a rich and complex belief system regarding death and the afterlife, blending heroic values, mythology, and practical rituals. Their beliefs were not strictly dualistic (heaven vs. hell), but rather included multiple afterlife realms depending on how a person lived and died. This religion also had roots much earlier, but like Shinto, it was organized and written down around the 7th century CE.

Valhalla was the hall of the slain. It was ruled by Odin, the chief of the gods. The Valkyries took warriors who died bravely in battle to Valhalla. There, they trained daily for rangarök, the final battle of the gods.

Feasting, drinking, and combat were central to the experience. It was eternal glory for the heroic dead. Half of those who died heroically went to Freyja's hall rather than Valhalla. It was a more peaceful afterlife, but still honored warriors.

The Realm of the Dead was governed by the goddess Hel, daughter of Loki. Souls of those who died from illness, old age, or without honor went there. Hel was not necessarily a place of punishment, but it was regarded as cold, shadowy, and joyless. The souls there were not punished but forgotten. Those who died at sea could go to Rán's realm, a sea goddess who caught the drowned in her net. Alternatively, they might reach Ægir's underwater halls.

The dead could return as spirits if they were dishonored, not properly buried, or angered. Some people believed in reincarnation within family lines, especially when names were reused. Ancestors were honored and sometimes consulted through seers or visions.

The **Tupi-Guarani** are among the most significant and widely spread Indigenous peoples of South America, especially in Brazil, Paraguay, Bolivia, and parts of Argentina. They form a large linguistic and cultural group composed of many tribes that speak related Tupi-Guarani languages.

They are part of the larger Tupi linguistic and cultural group, which began migrating into the Amazon and Atlantic Forest regions of South America from the Amazon Basin around two thousand years ago. By 1000 CE, distinct Tupi-Guarani cultures had established themselves extensively in the areas of present-day Brazil, Paraguay, Bolivia, and northern Argentina, with complex religious, social, and agricultural systems in place.

Their spiritual beliefs, including reverence for nature, ancestral spirits, and a belief in a spirit world, had been well developed by this time and were passed down orally from generation to generation. Unlike literate civilizations, their traditions weren't written down until after European contact. However, linguistic and ethnographic evidence support a deep-rooted and coherent belief system by at least 1000 CE, if not earlier.

The Tupi-Guarani had monotheistic tendencies. Some tribes believed in a supreme creator god. They believed everything in nature, including rivers, animals, and trees, had a spirit. Reincarnation and spiritual journeys were common beliefs. A strong emphasis on dreams, visions, and shamans, who were spiritual healers and guides. Many believed the soul continued on a journey, possibly to a paradise or through cycles of rebirth.

Around the same time, in approximately 1000 CE, the **Mapuche** religion emerged. The Mapuche are an indigenous people of south-central Chile and southwestern Argentina, with spiritual beliefs deeply rooted in nature, their ancestors, and the harmony of the world. Their traditional religion, sometimes called Mapuche spirituality or Admapu, combines animism, shamanism, and ancestor veneration.

The Mapuche believe that humans have a spiritual essence that continues after death. After passing away, the spirit travels to a spiritual realm, often referred to as the land of the dead. The soul's journey is guided by ancestors or spiritual beings. The afterlife isn't viewed as eternal bliss or torment but as a continuation of life in another realm, sometimes reflecting the earthly one. Maintaining harmony with nature and honoring one's ancestors is believed to facilitate a peaceful journey after death.

The **Inca** civilization started in the early 1200s CE and lasted until the Spanish conquest in 1533 CE. They lived mainly in the Andes Mountains of South America, with their capital in Cusco, which is now located in Peru. At its height, the Inca Empire extended along the Pacific coast and highlands from what is now southern Colombia, through Ecuador, Peru, Bolivia, and northern Chile, and into northwest Argentina.

The Inca held deep reverence for death, the afterlife, and ancestral spirits. They believed mortality was a transition into another realm, with rituals ensuring the deceased remained part of the living world. The Inca saw death as a transformation. The soul's journey led to one of three realms.

The upper world, which was much like heaven, was reserved for the virtuous and elite. Some spirits lingered to help the living in the mortal world. Others went to the underworld, which was connected with fertility and hidden forces. Souls might split apart. One part would ascend, while the other part remained with the mummy.

Royal and elite mummies were treated as if they were still alive. They were displayed, clothed, fed, and consulted on state affairs. They served as spiritual protectors, influencing politics, agriculture, and society.

Capacocha was a sacrifice of purity and was a major ritual involving the sacrifice of children, both elite and pure. This ritual was performed during significant events, such as the ascension of an emperor, disasters, and other important occasions. It was viewed both as offerings to gods and ancestors. It aimed to maintain balance in nature and in politics.

Although the **Aztec** civilization is closely tied to **Mesoamerican religions**, it emerged much later, roughly between 1300 and the Spanish conquest in 1521 CE. It was the state religion of the Aztec Empire.

The religion was polytheistic, with hundreds of gods associated with various aspects of nature, agriculture, war, and daily life. It was influenced by earlier Mesoamerican cultures such as the Olmec, Teotihuacan, and Toltec civilizations, and human sacrifice was believed to be essential for nourishing the gods and maintaining cosmic order.

The Aztecs believed the universe was structured around four sacred directions and layered across three realms. The three realms included the Overworld, the Earth, and the Underworld. Each of the four directions was associated with its own color, deity, and elemental power, symbolizing the balance that held creation together. Above and below the earthly plane, multiple levels stretched.

There were thirteen heavens rising toward the divine and nine underworlds descending into shadow, all interconnected by the great cosmic axis. Death, in Aztec thought, was not judged by morality but by the manner of one's death, which determined the soul's destination. Those who died in battle or were chosen for sacrifice were believed to ascend to the highest realms of the heavens, while others journeyed through the underworld's nine levels before reaching final rest.

The Aztecs are often remembered as one of the most blood-stained civilizations in history, even surpassing the Maya in the scale of their human sacrifices. Yet behind this reputation lay a profoundly structured and symbolic understanding of death and the afterlife. Their elaborate rituals were not acts of cruelty, but sacred duties meant to sustain cosmic balance by guiding souls through the underworld and preserving harmony between the realms of the living and the dead.

Destinations of the Soul depended on how a person died. If killed in battle, by sacrifice, or in childbirth, souls joined the sun's path and lived on as hummingbirds or gods of the sun. Others traveled to Mictlān, the underworld ruled by Mictlāntecuhtli and Mīctēcacihuātl. Journey to Mictlān involved a perilous four-year, nine-stage ordeal, including crossing rivers with a dog psychopomp, navigating fiery winds, jaguars, and frozen mountains.

Sikhism was founded in 15th-century Punjab by Guru Nanak and grew under the guidance of nine successive Gurus. From the sixth Guru onward, the community faced increasing persecution from Mughal authorities, who tried to suppress the expanding faith. In response, the tenth Guru, Guru Gobind Singh (1666–1708), formalized the Khalsa in 1699. It was an initiated Sikh order founded on high moral standards, equality, and willingness to fight injustice.

Sikhs in the Khalsa were taught to live an ethical life free from ego, as saint-soldiers devoted to God. The Khalsa, meaning "the pure" in Punjabi, is the community of initiated Sikhs who have dedicated themselves to living by the highest principles of Sikhism. These principles are courage, equality, discipline, and devotion to God.

Soldiers are courageous and armed, ready to protect anyone in danger, regardless of religion or background. A famous Sikh saying is "When all peaceful means have failed, it is righteous to draw the sword." This is why in history Sikhs often stood up for the oppressed, the outnumbered, and the defenseless, even for people who were not Sikh.

In Sikhism, death is seen not as an ending, but as a natural part of the soul's journey toward union with the Supreme Reality or God. Sikhs do not believe in heaven or hell in the traditional sense but in liberation from the cycle of birth and death through spiritual growth, ethical living, and remembrance of God.

Sikhs believe that the soul is eternal and reincarnates many times as part of the cycle of birth and death. When a person dies, the soul moves on based on its karma and spiritual condition. A spiritually enlightened soul merges with God, ending the cycle of rebirth.

The goal of a Sikh is liberation from the cycle of reincarnation. This is achieved not through rituals or renunciation, but by meditating on God's Name, living truthfully and righteously, and serving others. Sikhs are taught to accept death as the divine will. Excessive grief or mourning is discouraged. Instead, there is an emphasis on gratitude, remembrance, and inner peace.

Hawaiian religion is part of the larger Polynesian belief system. It spread across the Pacific as Polynesians migrated from Melanesia in Southeast Asia to Tahiti and then to Hawaii. Polynesian settlers likely reached the Hawaiian Islands between 300 and 800 CE, bringing their gods, oral traditions, and ritual practices with them.

Over the centuries, these beliefs evolved uniquely in Hawaii, shaped by the islands' environment and leadership structure. By the time Captain Cook arrived in 1778, Hawaiian religion had evolved into a complex, polytheistic system with strict and sacred laws.

Death was viewed as a transition rather than an ending. The spirit persisted after the body died. Its destination depended on how the person lived, their social status, and the rituals observed after death. There were two main paths.

First, they could return to the ancestors. Peaceful spirits could join their family's spiritual guardians, who protected the living. The second path led to wandering or malevolent spirits. The souls that were restless or vengeful. These spirits could trouble the living if they were not properly guided.

The Milky Way was regarded as the pathway of souls and was called "the black shining road of Kāne". Certain sacred cliffs, known as "leaping places of the soul," were believed to be where spirits leapt into the next world. Examples include Kaʻena Point in Oʻahu and Leina Kaʻuhane in Kauaʻi. Ancestors could return in dreams or as animal shapes, such as sharks, owls, or lizards, to guide and protect families.

In summary, there have been six monotheistic (belief in one God) societies in history. Monotheists generally reject reincarnation. However, Sikhism includes the concept of reincarnation until spiritual liberation is achieved. Most others believe in heaven or paradise for the righteous and hell for the wicked. Early Judaism thought the underworld was a shadowy place for all the dead before ideas of heaven and hell developed later.

There have been twenty-three polytheistic societies in our history. Of those, eleven believe in a physical or ancestral reincarnation. Seven believed in a bleak underworld, and five believed in a promised land or paradise.

Seven of the religions we have discussed are believed to hold additional beliefs. Some are unclear or have unknown details. One believed in both a joyful and dangerous Overworld, with reincarnation possible.

At least two believed in multiple heavens, hells, and ancestor realms. Others focused on moral legacy rather than specific afterlife concepts, and some believed that spirits stay connected to the living.

Of the four non-theistic religions, two believe in a cycle of endless rebirth until enlightenment or liberation. One focused on ancestral worship and had minimal beliefs about the afterlife. And of course, Atheism doesn't believe in any kind of spiritual afterlife.

Of the forty religions we have studied, all but atheism believe that the soul, life force, or life energy persists after death and continues to exist. So, where does it go?

Does it go to a bleak underworld with no pleasure, existing in nothingness? Does it go to a paradise if it is a righteous soul, or to a place of pain and suffering if it was a non-righteous soul? Or does it simply end, along with all that we have learned, experienced, and created, as atheists believe?

Let's explore further and see what the creation stories of these civilizations say not only about our origins but also about where the soul might return.

Chapter Six

Before we examine the creation stories of the religions discussed in previous chapters, I would like to clarify that when creation myths refer to "chaos" in the beginning, they're not referring to disorder in the everyday sense. It's more of a cosmic, primordial state that exists before the world, the sky, the earth, or life has formed. Think of it as the raw, unshaped potential of everything. It's like a blank canvas of existence, waiting for a creator or cosmic force to give it shape. Many myths describe chaos as water, mist, or darkness, representing fluidity, formlessness, or the unknown.

Chaos in creation myths is the primordial, undifferentiated state of existence. A raw, limitless potential from which the cosmos, life, and order are born. It's a symbolic way of saying: "Before there was anything we know, everything was possible, but nothing yet existed in form."

We don't have any direct evidence that **Neanderthals** had a *creation story* in the way later human cultures did. There's no preserved writing, oral tradition, or symbolic art that we can confidently connect to as myths about the origins of the world or humanity. As we discussed earlier, their burials, symbolic behavior, and possible language skills make it plausible they had some kind of mythic or spiritual explanations for life and death, but nothing survived to give us certainty.

Stories require a continuous oral chain. Once the Neanderthals became extinct around forty thousand years ago, any traditions they had would have died with them. Without writing, myths tend to vanish unless passed on to another culture, and there's no evidence that early Homo sapiens absorbed Neanderthal myths.

The **Australian Aboriginal Dreamtime,** also known as the Dreaming, is not just a single creation story but a vast collection of spiritual, moral, and historical knowledge. It is a living belief system that varies from one nation to another across the continent. Each Aboriginal group has its own creation stories, but they share common themes.

While there isn't a single "official" version, many Dreamtime stories follow a common pattern. In the beginning, the world was flat, dark, and empty. Ancestral beings, often in the form of animals, humans, or hybrid creatures, emerged from the earth, sky, or ocean. These beings shaped the landscape by creating mountains, rivers, waterholes, and plants. They also created people and endowed them with languages, laws, and customs. After finishing their work, they transformed into parts of the natural world, becoming stars, rocks, animals, or sacred sites.

There's also no single Indigenous North American creation story. Just like Australia, the continent had hundreds of distinct nations, each with its own language, culture, and spiritual beliefs. But many of these stories share recurring themes. The world emerging from water, creation by a Great Spirit, and animals playing important roles in shaping the earth.

The **San**, also known as Bushmen, reside in Southern Africa. They have many regional variations of their creation story, since their culture is one of the oldest continuous traditions on Earth. Some of their myths may go back tens of thousands of years. While the details differ between groups, there are common threads.

Their creation story features a First Creator, often seen as a deity in the tales. This deity is typically a shapeshifter, sometimes taking the form of a praying mantis or a man. The world originated from chaos. At first, it was dark, formless, and flat.

Many animals were once human, and shifting between human and animal forms was common. The Gift of Light and Death, along with the sun and moon, are introduced by the Creator or their family. Death entered the world due to a misunderstanding.

The **Mesopotamian** creation story primarily originates from the Babylonian text known as the Enuma Elish, which translates to "When on high," and dates back to around the late second millennium BCE but draws on much older Sumerian myths. It's not just a story about "how the world began," but also a political narrative explaining why the chief god, Marduk, deserved to rule over the other gods.

Before Earth, sky, or humans existed, there was only primordial water. Apsu is the sweet, fresh water and is male. Tiamat is the salty seawater and is female. These waters mingled, giving birth to the first generation of gods.

The younger gods became noisy and restless. Apsu wanted to kill them to restore peace, but Ea, or Enki, god of wisdom, killed Apsu first. Tiamat, enraged, created an army of monsters to avenge him and placed Kingu, her new consort, in command.

None of the gods could defeat Tiamat, so they offered Marduk, the storm god, leadership of all the gods if he would fight her. Marduk accepted, but only on the condition that he would be the only one given supreme power forever. Marduk trapped Tiamat in a net, shot an arrow into her heart, and killed her. He split her body in two.

One half became the sky, and the other became the earth. Marduk established constellations, created the calendar, and assigned gods to rule over natural elements. From Kingu's blood, mixed with clay, Marduk made humans. Their purpose was to serve the gods, thereby freeing them from labor.

Ancient Egypt didn't have just one creation story. Each major religious center had its own version, with different gods taking the lead. But all of them shared a basic theme. In the beginning, there was chaos, a watery void, and from it arose the first god, who created the world and other deities.

They all share the same premise that in the beginning, there were only dark waters and chaos. The first god emerged from the water, either self-created or rising from a primeval mound. He then brought the world into existence, either by creating the first divine pair of air and moisture or through thought and speech. "He conceived it in his heart and spoke it into existence."

The tricky part about the **Indus Valley Civilization**, located in what is now Pakistan and northwest India, is that we don't have a written creation story from them. At least, not one we can read.

Since no one has been able to read their writing, we don't know if the people of the Indus Valley had any written "holy books." What we do know comes from the clues they left behind, such as the famous Pashupati seal, small statues and figurines, city layouts, and what seem to be ritual baths. By examining these discoveries, researchers believe that their beliefs may have influenced later Hindu traditions, which might still carry traces of the ancient spirituality of the Indus people.

The **Canaanite religion** in modern-day Israel, Palestine, Lebanon, western Syria, and Jordan has a creation story preserved mainly through fragments of Ugaritic texts unearthed at Ras Shamra, now in modern Syria, in the 1920s and 1930s. These clay tablets, written in a cuneiform alphabet around 1400–1200 BCE, show a polytheistic worldview centered on a divine family led by the god El.

In the beginning, there was nothing but the endless, primordial waters. From these waters came two deities: Apsu, symbolizing fresh water, and Tiamat, representing the chaotic saltwater sea. Their story closely resembles the Mesopotamian creation myth, although the characters are described in somewhat different terms.

In the **Ugaritic version**, the first divine beings are El, the high god, and Asherah, his consort, often referred to as the "Lady of the Sea." From the mingling of these waters came the first generation of gods, who dwelled at the "source of the two rivers" and the "fountain of the deep." El, the father of gods and men, became the chief deity, ruling over the pantheon from his tent on a cosmic mountain.

The **Judaism** creation story comes primarily from the opening chapters of the Book of Genesis in the Hebrew Bible. It presents two closely related creation accounts that together form the Jewish understanding of how the world began.

Genesis 1:1–2:3.

Before creation, there was chaos. "The earth was formless and void, and darkness was over the surface of the deep."

Day one: God (Elohim) creates light, separating it from darkness (day and night).

Day two: God forms the sky, separating the "waters above" from the "waters below."

Day three: God gathers the waters to form seas, letting dry land appear, and creates vegetation.

Day four: God creates the sun, moon, and stars to govern day and night and mark seasons.

Day five: God creates sea creatures and birds.

Day six: God creates land animals and finally humankind (male and female) in His image, giving them stewardship over the earth.

Day seven: God rests, blessing the Sabbath as holy.

The creation stories of **Polynesian religions** vary from island to island, encompassing Tahiti, Hawaii, Samoa, Tonga, and Aotearoa (New Zealand). However, they share many core themes, such as the world emerging from primordial darkness or chaos, the role of sky father and earth mother, and the actions of gods or culture heroes who separate, shape, and populate the world. Here's a broad synthesis, with a well-known example from the Māori in New Zealand, and Hawaiian traditions to illustrate the pattern.

In the beginning, there was Darkness or Night. It was an endless void, often imagined as a womb containing the potential for life. Sky Father and Earth Mother were locked in a tight embrace, and their many children were trapped in darkness between them. The children, often gods representing natural forces such as the forest, sea, wind, and others, debated on how to bring light into the world. Once light and space existed, the gods created mountains, rivers, seas, and living creatures. Humans were often shaped from earth or sand.

The **Hindu** creation story from the Proto-Vedic period primarily originates from the Rigveda, one of the oldest sacred texts of Hinduism. Unlike the linear, single-author creation stories of some other cultures, the Rigveda offers multiple, sometimes conflicting, hymns and ideas about how the world came into being.

The universe begins in nonexistence or undifferentiated water/ chaos. There is no clear "first being" at the start. Instead, there is a cosmic potential, sometimes referred to as "Asat," or non-being, and "Tamas," which is darkness. Creation is accomplished through a Cosmic being who is sacrificed.

Some hymns, like the Nasadiya Sukta, "The Hymn of Creation," describe creation emerging from primordial waters, with the cosmic golden egg floating in the void. From this egg, the universe, gods, and living beings came into existence. Creation aligns with cosmic law or order called Rta. It's the principle that maintains balance in the universe. Humans, animals, and gods all exist within this order.

Mesoamerican religions, including those of the Olmec, Maya, and Aztec, each had its own creation myths, but they share common themes. The universe was created from primordial waters or chaos. The gods struggled to create humans, and humans were made to honor or serve the gods.

The **Zoroastrian** creation story originates from the teachings of Zoroaster and later texts, such as the Avesta. Zoroastrianism is one of the earliest monotheistic religions, emphasizing a cosmic battle between Ahura Mazda, the Wise Lord, and Angra Mainyu, the destructive spirit.

Before creation, there was only Ahura Mazda, pure, wise, and all-good, in an unchanging spiritual realm. Angra Mainyu, the destructive spirit, arises as an opposing force, representing chaos, lies, and evil. Ahura Mazda creates the material world as a battleground to defeat Angra Mainyu.

He creates the spiritual realm first, then the physical world, which includes the sky, earth, water, plants, animals, and humans. Humans are created as helpers of Ahura Mazda, capable of choosing truth or falsehood. The universe is structured around dualities. Good versus evil, light versus darkness, and order versus chaos.

Zoroastrian cosmology emphasizes a finite cosmic struggle. Ahura Mazda will ultimately triumph. There will be a resurrection of the dead, a final judgment, and a purification of the world. Ultimately, creation will be restored and perfected, and evil will be eliminated entirely.

The **Celtic (Proto-Celtic)** creation story is less formalized than the written myths of the Greeks or Mesopotamians. Most of what we know comes from later Irish and Welsh mythology, which preserves oral traditions of the early Celts. There's no single "Celtic creation epic," but scholars reconstruct some themes based on these later myths and archaeological evidence.

The world often begins as a watery or formless void, sometimes linked to cosmic wells or sacred lakes. Water and nature are sacred, reflecting the Celts' deep connection to rivers, forests, and the land. A pantheon of divine beings embodies natural forces, craftsmanship, magic, and fertility.

They arrive in Ireland, sometimes through mist or otherworldly travel, and shape the land. Humans are part of a cosmic balance, connected to animals, plants, and spirits. Creation is not a one-time event. Instead, the world is constantly shaped through interactions between gods and mortals.

Since the **Romans** borrowed heavily from Greek mythology, the Greek and Roman creation stories are closely related. The Greek myths, recorded in works like Hesiod's Theogony, c. 700 BCE, describe a succession of divine generations, with the world emerging from chaos and order established through conflict among gods.

In the beginning, there was Chaos, a formless void. From Chaos came the earth, the underworld, love, desire, night, and darkness. Gaia gave birth to the sky, mountains, and sea deities. Prometheus, a Titan, molded humans from clay. He stole fire from the gods and gave it to humans, angering Zeus.

Chinese folk religion is a broad, syncretic tradition that combines ancestor worship, animism, and later influences from Taoism, Confucianism, and Buddhism. Because it isn't centralized, there isn't just one creation story, but several mythic traditions explain the origins of the world. Two of the best-known are the Pangu myth and the Nuwa creation myth.

The **Panga** myth states that in the beginning, the universe was a cosmic egg or undifferentiated chaos. The egg splits into Yin (dark, feminine) and Yang (light, masculine). Inside the egg was Pangu, a giant being who grew for eighteen thousand years. He separated Yin and Yang completely, creating the earth, which is Yin, and the sky, which is Yang. He held them apart, growing taller as the sky rose. When Pangu died, his body transformed into the features of the world.

The **Yoruba** religion originated in the southwestern regions of Nigeria, Benin, and Togo. It is a polytheistic faith with a diverse pantheon of deities known as Orishas. Its creation myth centers on the supreme god Olodumare, also known as Olorun, and his delegation of creation tasks to lesser deities.

In the beginning, there was Olodumare, the supreme, eternal god, who existed in the heavens. The earth was a featureless watery void, often described as chaos or nothingness. Olodumare sent Obatala, an Orisha associated with purity, creation, and wisdom, to shape the earth.

Obatala molded humans from clay. Olodumare then breathed life into them, giving them spirits. Some humans were imperfect or malformed because Obatala became drunk while creating them, giving an explanation for human diversity.

The **Sámi** people are the indigenous people of northern Scandinavia and parts of Russia. Their spiritual traditions, often referred to as Sámi shamanism, are animistic and centered on nature, spirits, and the activities of shamans. Unlike written religions, their creation stories were passed down orally, so there isn't a single "canonical" narrative. However, scholars have reconstructed common themes.

In the beginning, there was darkness and water, sometimes described as a shapeless void. The Earth had not yet formed. Everything existed as spirit and potential. Spirits, goddesses, gods, and nature spirits inhabited the world even before humans. The Sun and Moon are powerful entities that guide life, but humans came later.

Spirits brought humans into the world, often from clay or earth, or by divine shaping from natural elements. Some stories say humans were created to help maintain harmony between nature and the spirit world. Shamans mediate between humans and spirits.

They ensure that humans respect the natural and spiritual order, often through rituals, drums, chanting, and journeys into the spirit world. Mountains, lakes, animals, and weather phenomena are all infused with spirit. Humans, spirits, and the natural world are interconnected, and balance must be maintained.

The **Zulu** and broader **Southern African** traditional religions are characterized as animistic and polytheistic, with creation stories that are passed down orally. These myths emphasize the role of a supreme creator, ancestral spirits, and the interconnectedness of humans, animals, and nature. In the beginning, there was a supreme creator, also called Unkulunkulu, who existed alone in the spiritual realm.

The earth was once formless, a void or watery chaos. Unkulunkulu descended to the earth and created land, mountains, rivers, and forests. He shaped animals, giving them roles in nature. Humans were formed by Unkulunkulu from clay or the earth. He endowed them with spirit and life, making them stewards of the natural world.

The **Taoist, or Daoist,** creation story originates in early Chinese philosophy and religious texts, particularly the Dao De Jing, attributed to Laozi (4th–3rd century BCE), and in later cosmological writings. Taoism doesn't feature a single dramatic narrative like many mythologies, but instead describes creation as a natural unfolding from the Tao (Dao), the ultimate, ineffable source of everything.

In the beginning, there was Tao, whose literal translation means 'the way,' an unmanifested, eternal principle. Tao is formless, infinite, and the source of all existence. It cannot be named or fully described. From the Tao comes the primordial chaos, a shapeless, undifferentiated state. This concept is similar to the idea of cosmic potential in other creation myths. Everything exists in potential but remains unformed.

From the chaos, Yin (dark, passive, feminine) and Yang (light, active, masculine) emerge. Their interaction brings movement, balance, and the dynamics of the universe. Heaven, Earth, and all things gradually emerge from the interaction of Yin and Yang. Mountains, rivers, plants, animals, and humans are formed naturally, following the Tao's flow.

Chapter Seven

Buddhism is unique among many other religions in that it does not have a single creation story. The Buddha focused on understanding suffering, called dukkha, impermanence, known as anicca, and the path to enlightenment, rather than explaining the origin of the universe. However, Buddhist texts do include cosmological ideas and sometimes describe the world in mythic terms.

Buddhism does not posit a supreme creator. The universe arises and ceases through natural, cyclic processes rather than divine will. Time is cyclical, with endless cycles of creation, existence, and destruction. These cycles apply to worlds, life forms, and beings, reflecting the impermanence of existence.

Buddhist texts describe multiple worlds and realms. The human realm, the animal realm, the hells, the heavens, and the realms of spirits. Beings are reborn in different realms based on their moral actions or karma. The Buddha discouraged speculation about the absolute origin of the universe, calling it unhelpful for achieving enlightenment. The focus is on understanding how suffering arises and how it can be ended.

Jainism is another religion that does not have a single "creation story" in the usual sense. Jain philosophy teaches that the universe has neither a beginning nor an end. It is eternal, uncreated, and operates according to its own natural laws.

The universe, known as Loka, has always existed and will continue to exist. There was no initial act of creation nor a supreme creator god. All existence consists of two eternal categories. The soul and living beings are infinite, conscious, eternal, and capable of liberation. Time moves in endless cycles, rising and falling like a wheel turning forever.

The periods of growth and progress are called Utsarpini, while the periods of decline are known as Avasarpini. Souls are bound by karma, which links them to the cycle of birth, death, and rebirth. Liberation (moksha) is achieved through nonviolence (ahimsa), truth, and ascetic discipline.

Jain texts describe the universe as shaped like a cosmic man or, alternatively, as a cosmic wheel. Gods and celestial beings exist, but they are not creators. They are also subject to karma and the eternal cycles of time. There are twenty-four enlightened teachers in each half-cycle of time, who rediscover and teach the eternal truths of Jain dharma when they are forgotten. The most recent is Mahavira, who lived in the 6th century BCE.

Instead of a creation story, Jainism teaches a cosmology of eternal cycles, where the universe has neither a beginning nor an end, and no external creator. Only infinite souls and matter that interact forever.

Confucianism also lacks a traditional creation story. Confucius, whose name was Kong Fuzi, lived from 551 to 479 BCE. Confucianism emphasizes ethics, morality, social harmony, and proper human conduct. It does not aim to explain the origin of the universe.

His teachings focus more on how to live well in the present than on cosmology or divine creation. However, Confucianism thought developed within a Chinese cultural context that included creation myths, mainly from Chinese folk religion and earlier philosophies.

If an ancient Chinese Confucian scholar discussed the origins of the world, they might have spoken of a giant who divided chaos into heaven and earth, or about the primal chaos from which yin and yang emerged, or possibly about a moral and ordering force that existed before humanity. But these were borrowed myths, not part of Confucianism's own doctrine.

The **Christian** creation story originates from the Bible's Book of Genesis (chapters one and two) and is central to Christian belief about God's role as Creator.

In the beginning, God created the heavens and the earth. The earth was formless and empty, and darkness was over the deep waters.

Day one: God created light, separating light from darkness — calling them "day" and "night."

Day two: God made the sky to separate the waters above from the waters below.

Day three: God gathered the waters to reveal dry land (earth) and created plants and vegetation.

Day four: God created the sun, moon, and stars to mark seasons, days, and years.

Day five: God created fish and other sea creatures, and birds of the air.

Day six: God created land animals and humankind — male and female — in His image, giving humans dominion over the earth.

Day seven: God rested, blessing the seventh day and making it holy.

Christians believe that God is eternal and created everything from nothing. Creation is good, as God declared everything he made to be "very good." Humanity is uniquely created in God's image, possessing spiritual, moral, and relational capacities.

The relationship between God, creation, and humanity is purposeful and moral. There is also Genesis two, which retells the creation story with a greater focus on humans. Adam was formed from dust, Eve from Adam's rib, and the Garden of Eden was their first home.

The **Ethiopian Orthodox Tewahedo Church** shares a similar creation story to mainstream Christianity, as its scriptures also begin with the book of Genesis. However, it also has unique emphases and additional traditions outside the Bible that are preserved in Ethiopian Christian literature.

Before anything existed, there was God, eternal, all-powerful, and alone. God willed creation into being out of nothing, not from pre-existing matter.

In **Islam**, the creation story primarily originates from the Qur'an and the Hadith, which comprise the sayings of the Prophet Muhammad. While it shares similarities with the Jewish and Christian Genesis stories, it has its own emphasis and details. Allah, God, has existed eternally, without beginning or end. Allah is the only Creator, and everything else is His creation. Nothing existed until Allah willed it into being. Allah created the heavens and the earth in six days. Periods of time were called Yaum and were not necessarily twenty-four hours long.

On the first days, the earth was shaped, and mountains were placed to stabilize it. Water, vegetation, and provisions for all living beings were created. The heavens were formed into seven layers (seven heavens) above the earth. Angels were created from light to serve Allah and carry out His commands. Jinn were created from smokeless fire, with free will. Some obey Allah, some disobey. Humans were the last major creation.

Allah formed Adam from clay, dust, and soil taken from different parts of the earth. This is why humans have different colors and temperaments. Allah shaped him, breathed his spirit (ruh) into him, and taught him the names of all things, thus giving humans knowledge that angels and jinn did not have.

Eve (Hawwa) was created from Adam. Islamic sources differ on the creation of Eve. Some say from Adam's rib. Others simply say from his "self." Either way, they were both placed in Jannah, which is a term for paradise, and told they could eat from anywhere except one specific tree.

Iblis, Satan, a jinn who had been among the angels, refused to bow to Adam out of arrogance when Allah commanded it. Iblis vowed to mislead humans until the Day of Judgment. He tempted Adam and Eve to eat from the forbidden tree. They disobeyed God's one rule and ate from the forbidden tree. They realized their nakedness and repented. Allah forgave them but sent them to live on earth as a test.

In Islam, there is no concept of original sin. Adam and Eve's sin is not inherited by others. Every person is born pure. Creation demonstrates Allah's power. The Qur'an uses creation as a sign of God's greatness. Humans are considered Khalifah or stewards on earth. Adam was made Khalifah or vicegerent to care for the earth.

Shinto is Japan's oldest spiritual tradition. Its creation story primarily originates from the Kojiki, known as the "Record of Ancient Matters," compiled in 712 CE, and the Nihon Shoki, compiled in 720 CE.

In the beginning, there was only chaos. From this chaos, heaven (known as Takamagahara in Japanese) and earth began to take form. Out of the heavens emerged several generations of kami, or divine spirits, known as the Kotoamatsukami, the heavenly deities.

Eventually, two important gods were born. Izanagi, whose name means "He Who Invites," and Izanami, meaning "She Who Invites." The elder gods gave them a sacred mission to create the land of the earth.

Shinto emphasizes that Japan is a sacred land. The islands are born from divine action, making the country itself a holy place. All aspects of nature have spiritual significance, and ritual cleanliness is essential for maintaining spiritual harmony.

The **Norse** creation story originates from Norse mythology. It is primarily preserved in the Poetic Edda and Prose Edda, which were the primary sources of the Vikings' and other Germanic peoples' religions before the spread of Christianity in Scandinavia. It's an epic tale of ice, fire, and giants.

In the beginning, there was Ginnungagap, a vast, empty void. To the north of Ginnungagap was Niflheim, the realm of ice, frost, and cold. To the south was Muspelheim, the realm of fire, heat, and light. The icy rivers from Niflheim met the sparks and heat from Muspelheim in the middle of Ginnungagap. The melting ice formed Ymir, a giant also called Aurgelmir, the ancestor of all frost giants. As Ymir slept, more giants were born from his sweat.

Along with Ymir, Auðhumla, a primordial cow formed from melting ice, arrived. Her milk fed Ymir. Auðhumla licked the salty ice blocks, and as she did, she uncovered Búri, the first of the gods.

Búri had a son named Borr, who married Bestla, a giantess. They had three sons. Odin, Vili, and Vé. Odin, Vili, and Vé killed Ymir. From his massive body, they created the world. His flesh became the land, his blood the oceans. His bones became the mountains, his teeth and broken bones the rocks. His skull became the sky, and was supported by four dwarves. His brain became the clouds.

While walking along the shore, Odin and his brothers found two tree trunks. They shaped them into the first man and woman. Ask, an ash tree, became the man. Embla, the elm tree, became the woman. Odin gave them life and a soul. Vili gave them intelligence and emotions. Vé gave them speech, hearing, and sight.

The world became Midgard, or "Middle Enclosure," a home for humans. Above was Asgard, the realm of the gods. Beneath was Helheim, land of the dead. The great World Tree, Yggdrasil, connected all realms.

The **Tupi-Guaraní** creation story comes from the Indigenous peoples of South America, mainly Brazil, Paraguay, and surrounding areas. It has several variations depending on the specific tribe and region, but the most well-known version centers on Tupã, the great creator.

In the beginning, there was only darkness and water. Tupã, the supreme god of light, descended from the heavens with his companion Arasy, the moon goddess. They landed on a high hill in what is now Paraguay. Tupã shaped the earth, the rivers, and the oceans. He created mountains, forests, and all the plants. He made the stars, the sun, and the moon to light the world.

From clay, Tupã molded the first man, Rupave ("Father of the People"), and the first woman, Sypave ("Mother of the People"). He gave them life, speech, and wisdom. Rupave and Sypave had many children who became the ancestors of all humans. Among their children were heroes and villains in Tupi-Guaraní legends.

Tupã also created the spirits of good to guide humans and the spirits of evil to tempt them. The most feared evil spirit was Anhanguera, "Old Devil", who brought suffering, disease, and death. The benevolent spirits encouraged love, courage, and respect for nature.

The Tupi-Guaraní believed that the soul would travel after death. The good and virtuous would go to a Land Without Evil called Yvy marane'ỹ, a paradise free from hunger, sickness, or death. The wicked would wander in darkness and misery.

The **Mapuche** creation story comes from the Indigenous Mapuche people of Chile and Argentina. It explains the origin of the world through a cosmic struggle between the forces of order and chaos.

In the beginning, there was no land, and the world was covered entirely by water. Two powerful spirits ruled this watery chaos. They were Tenten Vilu, the serpent spirit of the earth, protector of life, and Caicai Vilu, the serpent spirit of the sea, ruler of the waters.

Caicai Vilu became angry with humans for disrespecting nature. He sent enormous waves and floods to cover the land. Tenten Vilu rose up to save humans and animals, lifting the earth and mountains higher to protect them from the water. Their battle shaped the geography. Mountains, valleys, lakes, and islands were formed as the land rose and sank.

When the great floodwaters finally receded, dry land began to reappear once more, forming mountains, valleys, and scattered islands. Humans, animals, and spirits were among the few beings who survived, and life slowly began to return. Together, they repopulated and renewed the earth, bringing balance back to the world after the chaos of the flood.

The **Inca** creation story explains the origins of the world, humanity, and the Inca people, blending Andean myths with later imperial tradition. In the beginning, there was darkness and a vast, featureless void. The supreme creator god Viracocha emerged from Lake Titicaca, or sometimes from the sea. Viracocha created the sky, the earth, the sun, the moon, and the stars. He then shaped the first humans from stone.

The first humans displeased Viracocha, so he sent a great flood to wipe them out. Only two survived to repopulate the world. From sacred places called pacarinas, caves, springs, and mountains, new peoples emerged.

The **Aztec** creation story is a rich mythological cycle explaining the origin of the world, the gods, and humanity. The Aztecs believed the universe had undergone multiple creations and destructions, with each cycle culminating in a new sun, and the current world is the Fifth Sun.

Before the world existed, there was nothing but darkness and water, inhabited by gods. The Aztec cosmos had four previous worlds (suns), each destroyed by catastrophe. Jaguars destroyed the First Sun. Hurricanes destroyed the Second Sun. Fiery rain destroyed the Third Sun. Floods destroyed the Fourth Sun. Each world had its own human population that perished.

Sikhism, founded by Guru Nanak in the 15th century CE, does not have a traditional creation story like many other religions. Instead, Sikh teachings focus on God as eternal and beyond time.

God exists beyond birth, death, and time. God is the eternal creator, sustainer, and destroyer. The universe and all life are manifestations of God's will and divine energy (Hukam).

Sikh scriptures, *the Guru Granth Sahib*, poetically describe creation, highlighting that God spoke the universe into existence. Light, space, and life emerged through God's command. Everything in the universe connects and reflects God's creative power. The text doesn't offer a literal timeline or mention "first humans." Sikhism emphasizes understanding God, living righteously, and serving others rather than the specifics of creation.

The **Zulu and other Southern African** creation stories vary by community, but many share common themes about Unkulunkulu, the supreme creator, and the emergence of the world from chaos.

In the beginning, there was only Unkulunkulu, which literally means "the Great One," the eternal and all-powerful God. The world was dark, empty, covered in water, and devoid of humans, animals, and plants. Depending on the version, Unkulunkulu emerged from a reed or a hole in the ground.

He created the earth, the mountains, the rivers, and the trees. He also created animals, placing each in its proper place. Unkulunkulu made the first man and woman from clay or reeds. He breathed life into them, giving them the ability to speak, think, and reproduce. Humans were given the role of caretakers of the land.

The **Sámi (Lapp)** creation story comes from the indigenous Sámi people of northern Scandinavia. It is deeply connected to nature, the spirits, and the shamanic worldview.

In the beginning, there was darkness, water, and a vast emptiness. The world was shapeless, and spirits existed in the void. A great cosmic bird or reindeer, depending on the version, laid an egg or carried a world on its back, which became the earth. The first humans and animals emerged from this world, guided by spirit forces. Mountains, rivers, and forests were seen as infused with spirits (noaidi spirits) and sacred life.

Humans were placed on earth to live in harmony with the natural and spiritual worlds. Shamanic rituals, drumming, and trance journeys connect humans to spirits, ancestors, and the cosmic order.

Life and death are part of a continuous cycle, with spirits influencing both realms.

The **Polynesian** creation story comes from the oral traditions of the Polynesian islands, including Hawaii, Tahiti, Samoa, and Aotearoa/New Zealand. There are variations among islands, but a common thread is the emergence of the world from primordial darkness and chaos through the actions of the gods.

In the beginning, there was nothing but darkness and a watery void. Ranginui, Sky Father, and Papatūānuku, Earth Mother, were the first divine beings, locked in an eternal embrace, separating heaven and earth. Their children, the gods, grew frustrated by the darkness and lack of space.

Tāne, god of forests and life, pushed his parents apart, creating space for humans, plants, and animals. The light of day and the sky were revealed, and the world began to take shape. Some myths say that Tāne or other gods shaped humans from clay or red earth. Humans were given life and placed on the newly formed land to care for the earth and its resources.

The **Hawaiian** creation story originates in Hawaiian mythology, which is part of the larger Polynesian religious tradition and features its own distinctive gods and customs.

In the beginning, there was Po, the darkness, chaos, and void. From Po emerged Wākea, Sky Father, and Papahānaumoku, Earth Mother. Wākea and Papahānaumoku gave birth to islands, mountains, and landforms that became the Hawaiian Islands. They also gave birth to other gods, humans, and natural elements. Humans descended from the union of gods and divine ancestors.

They were placed on the islands to live in harmony with the land, sea, and the gods.

In summary, all the creation stories we have examined can be categorized into five distinct groups. The Greeks, Norse, Mesopotamians, Egyptians, Mesoamericans, and Taoists all believe that in the beginning, the world was a void or a state of chaos.

The Egyptians, the Mesopotamians, the Hindus, the Polynesian, and the Incas believed that in the beginning, there was water. However, it is worth noting that in creation myths, "water" does not necessarily refer to a literal ocean. It's a symbolic way of saying "shapeless nothingness" or "potential existence." So, in a sense, the water-origin myths overlap with the void/chaos myths.

Judaism, Christianity, Islam, Zoroastrianism, Sikhism, Taoism, and Confucianism believe that creation didn't start from chaos but from an eternal deity or principle that always was.

Australian Aboriginal Dreamtime, indigenous North American traditions, San, Yoruba, Zulu, and southern African, Sami Shamanism, Tupi-Guaraní, Celtic, and Hawaiian/Polynesian beliefs all include the idea that the world is shaped by spirits, culture heroes, or ancestors rather than chaos or a god.

Hinduism, Buddhism, Jainism, and atheism comprise the last group, which believes that there is no single beginning but rather eternal cycles or emanations.

What's remarkable about this correlation of creation stories is that, regardless of the distance between these cultures or their position in the historical lineage, they all developed the same basic creation stories, although the names of the gods varied.

Of the thirty religions and cultures we have looked at, eleven believed in nothingness and chaos, whether it was water or a void. Six believed in an eternal god. Nine believed that the ancestors or spirits created the heavens and the earth, and four believed there was no beginning, only eternal cycles.

So, what does this have to do with death and what happens to us after we die? So far, we have seen where the world's cultures believe we come from and where they believe we go when we die. These beliefs had to have developed somewhere. Whether it is divine intervention or imagination, all of these stories share many commonalities and tell a similar tale. There must be some truth to the stories, and logically, the similarities in all the stories during a time when there was no interaction among continental cultures, due to travel restrictions, suggest that imagination has to be ruled out.

Let's keep moving forward and explore more of life's mysteries. Doing so will help us unravel the mystery of death and help us understand what really happens when we die.

Chapter Eight

Many people have experienced near-death events. They claim to have had out-of-body episodes. They describe seeing a white light and feeling like family or friends are guiding them. Books have been written about this, and talk shows have featured many of these stories.

These experiences are commonly referred to as near-death experiences (NDEs). They are remarkably consistent across different cultures and historical periods, although interpretations differ. Here's a list of some of the most well-known near-death experiences on record, including the individuals' reported experiences during their moments of clinical death.

Dr. Eben Alexander, a neurosurgeon from the United States, wrote a book about his experience, titled *Proof of Heaven*. In 2012, Dr Alexander was clinically dead for seven days due to meningitis, a rare brain infection, and had no measurable brain activity.

He claims to have seen a vivid spiritual realm, including a beautiful girl guiding him. He later claimed she was his deceased sister, which was unknown to him at the time. He claimed he saw a "Core" presence, which he interpreted as God, and he felt a sense of infinite love, peace, and deep understanding.

Anita Moorjani from Hong Kong was a cancer survivor. She died in a hospital after slipping into a coma due to Hodgkin's lymphoma, an end-stage cancer. She experienced a realm of pure consciousness and light. She felt herself expanding beyond her body and experiencing unconditional love. She met her deceased father and said she had a choice to return or stay. When she chose life, her cancer rapidly disappeared. She published a book in 2012 titled "Dying to Be Me."

Howard Storm is a former atheist professor from the United States. He collapsed in Paris from a perforated stomach and was declared clinically dead before emergency surgery. He initially saw a dark void and malevolent beings who mocked and tormented him.

He cried out for help, and a being of light, which he believed was Jesus, rescued him. He was taken on a tour of the afterlife and shown the consequences of his actions as well as the purpose of life. After his experience, he became a Christian minister and wrote a book called *My Descent Into Death*.

Pam Reynolds from the United States is a well-documented case, caused by brain surgery. During a rare procedure to remove a brain aneurysm, her body was cooled to 60°F, and her heart and brain activity ceased completely for over an hour.

She reported observing her surgery from above the operating table, and hearing specific surgical tools and conversations that were later confirmed as accurate. She described entering a realm of light and love, where she met deceased relatives. She was told it wasn't her time and was sent back to her body. This case is considered one of the most medically documented NDEs ever.

Captain Dale Black was a commercial airplane pilot who survived a crash in Burbank, California. His plane went down in 1969, and he was clinically dead for minutes before being revived. He claimed to have visited heaven, experiencing colors, music, and peace beyond description. He instantly became aware of spiritual truths and divine love. Eventually, he was sent back with a renewed sense of purpose. He wrote about his experience in his book *Flight to Heaven,* published in 2010.

Don Piper was a car crash survivor from the United States. He was declared dead at the scene of a car accident for ninety minutes before being revived. He claimed to have visited the gates of heaven, where he was greeted by deceased loved ones. He described hearing music, feeling overwhelming love, and being turned away before entering fully. He wrote a book titled "Ninety Minutes in Heaven" about his journey to the afterlife.

Researchers and skeptics argue that near-death experiences are caused by other factors, not the afterlife. They point out that when the brain is deprived of oxygen, people can see tunnel vision, bright lights, and experience euphoria. Fighter pilots exposed to high G-forces sometimes describe tunnel vision and "out of Body" sensations, similar to near-death experiences. Therefore, to skeptics, the tunnel of light reported is simply the result of the eye and brain shutting down.

They also suggest that brain chemistry and neurotransmitters play a role in the near-death experience. Endorphins and other chemicals like serotonin, dopamine, or DMT may flood the brain during trauma, creating feelings of peace, love, or visions.

Some drugs like ketamine and DMT can induce hallucinations nearly identical to near-death experiences, with reports of floating, traveling through tunnels, and seeing beings of light. They go further to claim near-death experiences are drug-like hallucinations triggered by stress.

DMT stands for Dimethyltryptamine. It's a naturally occurring psychedelic compound found in certain plants, like ayahuasca, and in trace amounts in animals and humans. When smoked or injected, it produces intensely vivid, short-lived hallucinatory experiences, and people have reported traveling through a tunnel or vortex of light.

They have also reported feelings of leaving their bodies, encounters with beings of light, entities, or guides, and a sense of timelessness. Some have reported merging with the universe and experiencing life-changing spiritual insights similar to those described in near-death experiences.

The question of whether DMT is produced in the human brain remains a topic of debate. Some studies suggest that the pineal gland, a small gland in the brain often referred to as the "third eye," may produce DMT.

In a 2019 study, researchers found that rodents' brains release DMT in measurable amounts, especially during stress or near death.

This led to the hypothesis that perhaps humans also release DMT at death, causing the near-death experience. As of now, scientists have not proven that humans release DMT during death.

Some researchers and experiencers believe DMT doesn't "cause" hallucinations but rather opens a gateway to another level of consciousness. This is similar to how near-death experience researchers argue that even if DMT is involved, it may be the mechanism the brain uses to access another dimension of reality.

Skeptics and researchers also argue that stimulation of the temporal lobe can produce the near-death experience. Electrical stimulation of the temporal lobe can cause out-of-body experiences, a sense of presence, or life-review visions.

In the 1980s and 1990s, Canadian neuroscientist Dr. Michael Persinger of Laurentian University developed an apparatus nicknamed the "God Helmet." It was actually a modified snowmobile helmet fitted with magnetic coils that generated weak, complex electromagnetic fields over specific areas of the brain, especially the temporal lobes.

Persinger hypothesized that religious or spiritual experiences, like sensing a divine presence, seeing visions, or feeling one with the universe, might be linked to electromagnetic activity in the brain, particularly in the temporal lobes. He believed that artificially stimulating these regions might lead people to experience sensations similar to those described in mystical or near-death experiences.

Many volunteers (Persinger claimed about eighty percent) reported sensations such as feeling a "presence" in the room, a sense of being watched or accompanied by another being, intense emotions of awe, fear, or peace, and altered states of consciousness similar to meditation or prayer Some even described it as feeling God-like presences, hence the nickname "God Helmet."

Not everyone could replicate Persinger's results. Later studies, notably by Swedish researchers Granqvist et al. (2005), found that when participants were unaware of the experiment's purpose, they didn't experience anything unusual. This suggested that expectation and suggestion might have played a large role.

Moreover, the magnetic fields were extremely weak, far below what is typically needed to directly influence neurons, so many neuroscientists remain skeptical that the helmet itself caused the experiences.

Despite the controversy, Persinger's work sparked ongoing research into the neurology of spirituality and how brain activity might shape religious or mystical perception. The "God Helmet" remains a symbol of the intersection between neuroscience, consciousness, and spirituality.

Skeptics have also referenced Rapid Eye Movement Intrusion and Sleep Paralysis. In this theory, near-death experience-like states can happen when REM sleep intrudes into waking consciousness. This may result in feelings of floating, paralysis, tunnel vision, and encounters with supernatural beings. Because of this, skeptics argue that near-death experiences could be dream-like states during a medical crisis.

Other critics will also argue that culture, religion, and expectations shape near-death experiences. Christians see Jesus or angels. Hindus sometimes report meeting Yama, the god of death. Buddhists may describe karmic visions. In their view, life reviews may be a kind of memory flashback distorted by stress.

And finally, other skeptics argue that near-death experiences aren't actually death. They claim that people who report such experiences weren't truly dead and that their brains were still active. Medical "flatline" doesn't always mean there's no brain activity. Subtle activity can continue for minutes. According to them, near-death experiences occur in the dying brain, not after death.

Their explanation for "Veridical" near-death experiences, where someone sees accurate events while unconscious, is that patients may have overheard medical staff or reconstructed the memory after waking. Sometimes, details were vague and were filled in after being told what had happened.

Feelings of peace and love are attributed to the reduction of pain and fear through the release of endorphins. Brain imaging shows that out-of-body experiences can be recreated by stimulating certain brain regions, especially the right angular gyrus.

Chapter Nine

The most well-documented cases of reincarnation come from Dr. Ian Stevenson and others who followed his research model. These cases are particularly compelling because they often involve young children with verifiable memories of people who had died before they were born. Here are some of the most famous and credible reincarnation case studies to date:

James Leininger was a boy born in 1998 who claimed memories of being a World War II pilot named "James." At the age of three, he would draw planes being shot down. He knew the name of the aircraft was the "Corsair," which is a World War II fighter plane. He said he flew the plane from the Natoma Bay and was shot down by the Japanese. He even gave the name "Jack Larsen" as a friend.

The USS Natoma Bay was a real World War II carrier. A pilot named James Huston Jr. died in a mission just as James had described. Jack Larsen, a real pilot from the ship, confirmed the mission. Independent researchers verified the information through military records, interviews, and historical documents.

Shanti Devi was a girl from Delhi, India, who was born in 1926. She recalled her previous life as a woman named Lugdi Devi, who died during childbirth. She described her home and husband in Mathura, a town she had never visited. She also provided the name and details of her past-life husband, as well as information about her house, utensils, and past events.

When investigators took her to Mathura, she recognized her former husband, his relatives, and places she'd never visited. The husband confirmed that the private conversations and personal details were things only Lugdi Devi would know. Even Mahatma Gandhi showed interest, and a government commission verified the accuracy of her memories. This case is considered one of the strongest examples of reincarnation in India.

Swarnlata Mishra was a woman from Katni, India. At the age of three, she began describing a life in Katni, including a different family. She recalled specific details about a home and family that had lived in Katni. She named relatives and described the house layout. She recognized family members and used pet names known only to the family.

Dr. Ian Stevenson documented this case and interviewed both families. As proof, he offered that she identified the house during a random city visit and that the former family confirmed all the names and inside jokes. This was a detailed, verifiable memory with no chance of prior exposure.

Imad Elawar lived in Lebanon and claimed a past Life in a nearby village. At age five, he claimed to have lived in a nearby town as a man named Ahmad. He identified Ahmad's family members, the layout of the house, details of a radio, and the cause of death. Dr. Stevenson located a deceased man named Ahmad, whose life matched Imad's claims in fifty-plus details. Some errors were found, but most were highly accurate and specific. A strong case from outside India, adding cross-cultural weight.

Purnima Ekanayake was a girl born in Sri Lanka with unusual birthmarks that looked like burns. She said she remembered being a man who had died in a car fire. She recalled the man's name, the location of the accident, his wife, and his children. She also described details of the crash and the clothes he was wearing.

As proof, it was offered that a man had died in a car fire nearby before she was born. The family confirmed all names, relationships, and details of the accident. Her birthmarks matched burn injuries on the deceased. This was a case that combined both physical evidence and an accurate memory.

Gus Taylor was born in the United States. When he was eighteen months old, Gus said he was his own grandfather named Augie. He recognized a photo of Augie's sister, who had died young and was never talked about by the family. He also identified Augie's car and favorite places.

The family confirmed he had never heard about the sister before and described events and objects from decades earlier. Although there is less evidence than in other cases, it was still compelling within the family.

Jenny Cockell was born and raised in England. From childhood, she had memories of being Mary Sutton, a mother in early 20th-century Ireland. Mary Sutton had died young, leaving several children behind. As an adult, Jenny tracked down Mary's children, described her life, and knew things only the real mother could.

The children immediately believed her, and she built emotional connections with them. She found the right village and identified the home and family without any prior access to records. This is a rare case of adult reincarnation, supported by both strong emotional and factual evidence.

Of course, skeptics have spent considerable time critiquing these stories. They argue that most strong claims of reincarnation originate from cultures that already hold such beliefs (India, Sri Lanka, Myanmar, Lebanon, etc.). They also contend that children may pick up ideas from family, community, or religion and then incorporate them into their memories.

They also believe that a child, no matter how young, may overhear details of someone else's life and later "remember" them as if they were their own. They also point out that parents sometimes ask leading questions or interpret vague statements as proof.

In many cases, they argue, records of the "previous life" are incomplete, and when matching the child's statements to a deceased person, it may not be as accurate as it appears. They also mention that reporting is selective. Hits are remembered, while misses are ignored.

Psychological explanations have also been suggested. They argue that a child's imagination, combined with a need for attention, can play a role. Some psychologists view reincarnation memories as a form of confabulation, in which the brain fills in memory gaps with invented details.

Others, however, claim outright fraud. They believe that, although rare, it's possible some families may exaggerate or fabricate these stories for attention, prestige, or financial gain.

When specifically asked about Stevenson and Tucker's research, they admit the cases are intriguing and unusual, but not definitive proof. The strongest critique is the absence of controlled environments. By the time researchers arrive, the family may have already shaped the story.

Philosopher Paul Edwards suggested that Stevenson's cases might be explained without resorting to reincarnation, primarily through cultural suggestion and memory errors. Skeptics don't deny the stories exist, but they argue they can be explained through psychology, culture, and human error rather than literal past lives.

And what about hauntings or ghosts? Is it possible that, instead of being reincarnated, a soul could end up in Purgatory, condemned to walk the Earth forever? What can be said about them?

The **Tower of London** in England is where Anne Boleyn was beheaded in 1536. She is most often seen in the Chapel of St. Peter ad Vincula, where she is buried. Guards have reported seeing her specter walking the halls with her severed head in hand.

It's also where Lady Arbella Stuart, a cousin of James I, was imprisoned for marrying without permission. She died mysteriously in her cell and is said to drift through the Queen's House.

Edward V and his younger brother Richard were confined in the tower by their uncle, Richard, Duke of Gloucester, who soon proclaimed himself King Richard III. They disappeared in 1483. Centuries later, two small skeletons were discovered. People claim to see childlike shadows in the Bloody Tower and hear giggling voices at night.

Other phenomena in the tower include phantom bears linked to the menagerie that was once kept there, sudden icy chills, and guards quitting after terrifying nighttime encounters.

Skeptics argue that the numerous "sightings" likely stem from the power of suggestion. People expect to see ghosts in such a bloody place, so they often do. The stories of Anne Boleyn and the "Princes in the Tower" have been retold for centuries. Skeptics argue that these tales might have influenced people's experiences, rather than actually involving a real spirit.

However, over the centuries, multiple Yeoman Warders, also known as Beefeaters, have sworn they have seen Anne Boleyn's apparition. Sometimes with her head tucked under her arm.

Skeptics say that Guards on long night shifts might experience fatigue, stress, or tricks of light in the stone halls. However, these are military men with reputations at stake. Several of these incidents have led to men resigning or refusing night duty. While they could have imagined it under stress, skeptics struggle with multiple independent accounts matching across decades.

The **Paris Catacombs** in France feature over two hundred miles of underground tunnels, lined with walls made from human skulls and bones. In the 1960s, a video camera was discovered deep within the tunnels, having been dropped by a man who'd been exploring.

His body wasn't discovered until years later, but his panicked final moments were captured on film. He appeared lost, disoriented, and running.

Visitors have reported hearing echoing voices and whispers with no apparent source. They also feel as if they are being followed, even though they are alone. The lights suddenly go out, forcing explorers to navigate in darkness, surrounded by bones. Some say secret cults still gather in hidden chambers of the catacombs, performing rituals among the dead.

Skeptics argue that the underground tunnels are naturally eerie, dark, damp, echoing, and claustrophobic. Hallucinations, panic attacks, and disorientation are common. As for the "Lost Man" video, skeptics point out that fear and lack of oxygen could cause disorientation, explaining why explorers sometimes die in the tunnels without supernatural causes.

Chloe the Slave lived on The Myrtles Plantation in Louisiana. Her master, Clark Woodruff, forced her to become his mistress. When she was caught eavesdropping on Clark, one of her ears was cut off as punishment. After that, she reportedly wore a green turban to cover the injury.

Hoping to regain favor with the family, she baked a cake with crushed oleander leaves, intending to make them ill so she could nurse them back to health and regain their trust. But the plan backfired. Instead of sparing their lives, the family, Sara Woodruff, and two of her children died from the poison. The other enslaved people, fearing retaliation, blamed Chloe for the deaths. To protect themselves, they supposedly lynched her, hanging her and throwing her body into the Mississippi River. Her turbaned ghost has appeared in photos and to visitors.

Other spirits seem to inhabit the grounds as well. A Native American woman is often seen wandering the grounds. A murdered overseer has been spotted pacing the veranda. Children laughing, running, and pulling pranks have been reported, and guests say they've felt small hands tug at their clothes. Recurring phenomena have also been reported, such as doors opening on their own, bedsheets being pulled off sleepers, and mirrors with unexplained handprints.

Skeptics claim that historians have found no records of Chloe, the poisoned cake, or the family murder legend. They suggest that the story may have been invented in the 20th century to attract tourists. They argue that the plantation's tragic history of slavery primes visitors to expect dark presences.

However, in the 1990s, a photo taken at the plantation appeared to show a figure of a woman standing between buildings where no one had been. Kodak experts analyzed the original film and said it hadn't been tampered with. So, while skeptics say it's shadows or light, the figure has features, including a face and a clothing outline that are difficult to explain.

The **RMS Queen Mary,** permanently docked in Long Beach, California, sailed from 1936 to 1967 and is now a floating hotel and museum. She is equally famous as one of the most haunted places in the world. She has carried over two million passengers and eight hundred thousand troops during her career as a luxury liner and troopship.

During World War II, when the RMS Queen Mary was used as a troopship, nicknamed the "Grey Ghost," a young sailor was killed when a watertight door, often called door thirteen, in the engine room crushed him. People have reported seeing a greasy figure in overalls near the scene, sometimes disappearing suddenly.

Although the pool rooms were drained decades ago, people still hear splashing and see wet footprints leading nowhere. A little girl named "Jackie" is often heard calling for her mother, laughing, or singing. EVPs or recorded ghost voices are often associated with her.

Cabin B340 is one of the most haunted rooms on the ship. Guests have reported sheets being torn away, faucets turning on by themselves, and strange voices and knocks coming from the walls. The activity was so intense that the cabin was sealed off for years. Other sightings have included a woman in 1930s swimsuits, a "lady in white" gliding through the ballroom, and the faint sound of orchestra music.

Skeptics say that the ship is old, with steel hulls that carry sound strangely. Creaks, bangs, and drafts are easily mistaken for paranormal activity. They will point to psychological suggestion, as many visitors are told ghost stories before taking the tour. So they interpret natural events as hauntings. Regarding the wet footprints by the pool? They claim condensation or visitors' shoes can explain those. And cold spots? They say those are common on old ships with uneven ventilation.

However, even skeptics are at a loss when it comes to recordings made by paranormal investigators of strange audio captured when the ship was empty. These include voices, knocks, and even the sound of children laughing. Some recordings respond directly to questions, which is harder to explain as random noise. Audio anomalies can be interference, but direct responses are more difficult to dismiss.

Skeptics also acknowledge that the mystery remains unsolved in certain situations where evidence is more difficult to dismiss. In 1936, two photographers from Country Life magazine, Captain Hubert Provand and Indre Shira, were photographing **Raynham Hall**. On the grand staircase, they reported seeing a misty figure descending. They captured what has become one of the most famous ghost photographs ever taken. A semi-transparent figure resembling a woman in a flowing gown.

The ghost is believed to be Lady Dorothy Walpole, who lived from 1686 to 1726. She was the sister of Britain's first prime minister, Robert Walpole. She married Charles Townshend, the second Viscount Townshend, who was known for having a violent temper. According to the story, when he found out Dorothy was unfaithful, he locked her away in Raynham Hall. She died there in 1726 under mysterious circumstances, and locals claimed her spirit remained in the house.

Witnesses describe her as a woman wearing a brown brocade dress, with empty or glowing eye sockets, and a pale face. Sightings of her began in the 19th century, with several guests and staff at Raynham Hall claiming to see her wandering the staircase and halls.

Skeptics argue the photo could have been made using double exposure, there could have been a smudge on the lens, or it was staged. However, the photo was taken by professionals, using 1930s equipment, and passed authenticity checks by photo experts of the time. It remains one of the most famous unexplained ghost photos.

The **Enfield Poltergeist** took place at 284 Green Street, Enfield, London. It spanned from August 1977 to 1979. It involved a single mother, Peggy Hodgson, and her four children. The disturbances primarily focused on the two daughters, Janet, aged eleven, and Margaret, aged thirteen. Witnesses reported that furniture was moving on its own, chairs were sliding, and tables were tipping over. Knocking sounds were heard on the walls and ceilings. Objects such as toys, marbles, and Lego bricks were thrown across rooms.

Janet spoke in a deep, growling voice, claiming to be a man named "Bill." She also levitated from her bed and was photographed by investigators in mid-air. Cold spots, electrical disturbances, and mysterious voices were recorded on tape.

The Society for Psychical Research (SPR) sent Maurice Grosse and Guy Lyon Playfair, who had documented hundreds of incidents. Several police officers, neighbors, and reporters also claimed to have witnessed strange events firsthand. The case drew heavy media attention in Britain.

Some investigators believed much of it was child mischief. Janet and Margaret were caught faking some incidents. However, skeptics admit that not all phenomena have been explained, such as independent witnesses hearing knocks or seeing objects move. Critics argue that stress, media attention, and psychological factors fueled the hysteria.

The case remains unresolved. It is a mix of genuine paranormal claims and proven hoaxes. It has inspired books, documentaries, and even Hollywood productions: The Conjuring 2 (2016) dramatized the events. Janet Hodgson later admitted to faking some activity but insisted that "not everything was faked. It was real."

Chapter Ten

The **Book of Enoch** is an ancient Jewish writing that was once highly influential but was omitted from most versions of the Bible. However, it is still included in the canon of the Ethiopian Orthodox Church. It is traditionally attributed to Enoch, the great-grandfather of Noah. It's a composite work written between the 3rd century BCE and the 1st century CE, containing several sections, including the Book of the Watchers, the Book of Parables, the Astronomical Book, and the Book of the Dead.

The Book of the Watchers describes how angels, also known as the "Watchers", descended to earth, corrupting the human race. They lusted after human women and fathered the Nephilim, a hybrid of human and angelic descent described as giants. These angels also taught humans forbidden knowledge of weapons, sorcery, and astrology.

God sends the archangels Michael, Gabriel, Raphael, and Uriel to punish the Watchers and their offspring. The fallen angels are imprisoned in a deep abyss until judgment, and Enoch is taken on journeys through heaven and earth, witnessing visions of cosmic secrets.

The Book of Parables/Similitudes introduces the figure of the "Son of Man," a messianic figure who sits on God's throne, judges the wicked, and vindicates the righteous. It also describes the final judgment, resurrection, and a kingdom of righteousness.

The Astronomical Book provides a detailed account of celestial bodies, calendars, and the cosmic order. It describes how the sun, moon, and stars move, reflecting an effort to align astronomy with divine law.

The Book of Dreams contains two visions. One vision describes the Great Flood, and the other presents Israel's history up to the coming messianic kingdom symbolically through animal allegories, where humans are represented as animals, Israel is shown as sheep, and oppressors are depicted as beasts.

The Epistle of Enoch includes ethical teachings and warnings about the fate of sinners. It describes ten future "weeks" of history culminating in the final judgment, with the righteous promised eternal blessings and the wicked facing destruction.

Was secret heavenly wisdom revealed to Enoch? Did he see both the beginning as well as the end? And what about the societies before them? Was there some kind of divine intervention that explained to them how the world was created and what the afterlife held?

So what really happens when we die? Are we reincarnated? Do we go to a paradise or to a dark underworld? Did we originate from chaos? From nothingness? From an abyss that could be described as water? And where are we as a race going? Are we evolving into something greater, or will we remain static in this reality forever?

Scientists and skeptics alike agree that ancient people depicted only things they saw or experienced on cave walls. To them, imagination had nothing to do with the ancients' thoughts. So, how did they know where we came from? How did they know where we went? What if they were all correct, and where we are heading is completely in our control?

In 1859, the British naturalist **Charles Darwin** published *The Origin of Species*. According to his book, over billions of years, life began as a single organism in the salty oceans. Through those billions of years and millions of mutations, all life forms have spawned as we know them today.

It doesn't matter if you believe in Darwinism or in the creationist theory of God creating the human species. There can be no denying that we as a species are evolving. But how are we evolving, and what are we evolving into?

If you look back through the fossilized record of man, there's one thing that stands out. Whether two thousand, two hundred thousand, or six million years ago, our basic attributes have remained largely unchanged.

We may have less hair and softer faces. We might be taller and walk more upright, but our body parts remain the same. Our basic structure, including our reproductive systems, has stayed essentially unchanged. Since humans first appeared on this planet nearly six million years ago, we and all our subspecies have had two arms, two hands, two legs, two feet, a head, and a torso.

It would be safe to say that, since Homo sapiens appeared around two hundred thousand years ago, we look similar to them and, in many cases, they resemble our parents, brothers, sisters, or friends.

There is, however, one of our attributes that has changed more than the others. Our skulls have undergone more significant changes than any other adaptations we have experienced. It is larger. It contains more mass and more space for a bigger brain. This has enabled us to transition into the technological age we are familiar with today.

Never before has there been an age in history with the comforts we enjoy today. If you had been a king two thousand years ago, your quality of life would not have matched ours. Nights would have been cold, and days would have been hot. The average lifespan was shorter due to medical issues now easily cured. Our food supply chain lets us enjoy foods that kings of the past couldn't even imagine. Today, we carry the world's knowledge in our phones.

So what are we evolving into? Does evolution affect only the physical attributes of a being, or could we be evolving in a different way? Could we be evolving spiritually, mentally, cosmically, and in a connected way? Could the soul, or the living energy we carry with us, hold the key to what we're evolving into? Are we running out of time to become what we're meant to be?

In 1901, **Dr. Duncan MacDougall**, a physician in Massachusetts, hypothesized that if the soul exists, it must have mass. He built a special bed placed on a sensitive scale to weigh patients dying from tuberculosis. He had six terminally ill patients placed on the scale as they died. He claimed that in the moments just after death, there was a sudden weight loss of about twenty-one grams or three-quarters of an ounce. He concluded this must be the weight of the human soul leaving the body. He later tried the same experiment with fifteen dogs and reported no weight loss, reasoning that animals had no souls.

Even then, his work faced criticism for being deeply flawed. The skeptics pointed out the small sample size, comprising only six human patients and fifteen dogs. Of the six humans, only one experienced weight loss that supported his claim. The others had conflicting results. Some lost weight slowly, some not at all, and one even gained weight.

They also claim that the equipment was unreliable. Scales in 1901 were not precise enough to detect subtle changes in weight, particularly in patients who were dying and moving. Patients thrashing, shifting, or fluids moving in the body could easily affect readings.

Physiological explanations, such as air leaving the lungs, sweating, the release of urine or feces, or simple shifts in body temperature and moisture, could account for weight fluctuations. The "sudden" loss could also simply be the body expelling its last breath.

They also believed MacDougall already wanted to prove the soul had mass, and dismissed results that didn't fit, including most of his own data. Additionally, there are ethical concerns because he experimented on dying patients without genuine consent standards. In the early 1900s, medicine had few protections.

Skeptics argued that scientists, both then and since, have stated that his results were neither repeatable nor scientific and were full of alternative explanations. No recent replication efforts have ever provided evidence that the body loses twenty-one grams at death. The idea that "twenty-one grams = the soul" mostly persisted as a popular myth, rather than a scientific discovery.

There have been some modern attempts, or at least claims, to "update" Duncan MacDougall's 1901 twenty-one gram experiment. Although they have not been scientifically validated, they are worth considering. A few researchers have attempted to redo MacDougall's idea using more precise scales.

These modern scales can measure milligrams, yet no one has observed a mysterious twenty-one-gram soul mass. There is no consistent weight loss at death beyond what can be attributed to the release of air from the lungs, evaporation of moisture, relaxation of the bladder and bowels, and changes in circulation that occur when the heart stops.

In the 1970s, some fringe researchers attempted to use **Kirlian photography**, which captures an electrical discharge image, to demonstrate that "life energy" leaves the body at the time of death. They claimed that the aura dims or disappears at the moment of death.

Skeptics argued that Kirlian images are just electrical discharges caused by moisture and do not prove the existence of souls. Controlled experiments have shown that the "aura" changes in response to humidity, pressure, or sweat, rather than to consciousness.

A few studies have pointed infrared cameras at dying patients or animals, claiming to detect a sudden burst of heat or light emanating from the body. The skeptics quickly responded that when the heart stops, blood flow ceases, and heat redistributes rapidly. This can create localized bursts of infrared light that seem mysterious but are actually a result of physics.

In the late 20th century, some Soviet and Eastern European labs conducted research on "biofields." The term "biofield" is a modern, scientific-sounding term that some researchers and practitioners use to describe the energy fields said to surround and permeate living beings. Even though mainstream science doesn't universally accept it, it is often linked to traditional ideas.

Prana is a concept from Hinduism and Yoga that refers to the universal life force or vital energy that flows through all living beings. Within the body, this energy moves through subtle channels known as nadis. Practices such as breathwork and meditation are used to guide and balance prana, promoting physical and spiritual well-being.

Chi (or Qi) originates in China, Taoism, and traditional Chinese medicine, and refers to the vital energy flowing through pathways, or meridians. Practices such as acupuncture, tai chi, and qigong aim to balance and guide chi. Ki comes from Japan's Reiki and is similar to chi, which is a form of energy that can be directed for healing.

The **soul or spirit** is a concept from Western tradition. It is sometimes seen as the life force that animates, although it is more often described in spiritual rather than energetic terms.

In modern discussions, biofields are described as subtle, dynamic electromagnetic fields generated by the body. They are possibly related to heart rhythms. The heart produces a strong electromagnetic field, along with brain waves and cellular activity.

This provides a way to bridge traditional "vital energy" concepts with scientific language.

The **U.S. National Institutes of Health** (NIH) has even used the term "biofield" in research on complementary and alternative medicine, although the scientific evidence is mixed and sometimes controversial.

They employed electromagnetic sensors and gas-discharge visualization. The results showed interesting signals around living organisms, but all of these could be attributed to normal biological processes, such as electrical activity in nerves and moisture on the skin.

Instead of focusing on measuring weight, some hospitals, like Dr. Sam Parnia's AWARE study, attempted to place hidden images or text on high shelves in resuscitation rooms so that only someone "floating" above their body could see them. Among the thousands of cardiac arrest patients interviewed, some reported vivid experiences, but no one has successfully identified the hidden targets. No modern experiment has demonstrated any mysterious weight loss, light bursts, or energy that cannot be explained by biology.

Chapter Eleven

The **parallel universe,** or multiverse, theory isn't primarily a spiritual or afterlife concept, but some people associate it with death in speculative ways. Hugh Everett proposed this idea in 1957. It states that whenever a quantum event occurs, reality "splits" into multiple universes. One for each possible outcome. According to this theory, all possibilities exist somewhere.

In one universe, you die at a certain moment. In another universe, events unfold differently, and you survive. From your own perspective of consciousness, you only experience the realities in which you remain alive. Some refer to this idea as "quantum immortality."

Some thinkers propose that because consciousness always unfolds in a timeline, it never truly experiences death. Instead, you "shift" into a branch of the multiverse where you survive, even if it's unlikely. To others in that universe, you may have died, but your subjective experience remains uninterrupted.

Physicist Max Tegmark described this in a thought experiment. Imagine a machine connected to a quantum event, like radioactive decay. If the particle decays, the machine fires a gun at you. If not, nothing happens.

From an outside observer's perspective across different universes, sometimes you live, sometimes you die. But from your perspective of consciousness, you only ever experience the universes where the gun doesn't fire. Therefore, subjectively, you never experience death. You always wake up in the branch where you survive.

You die in most universes, from other people's point of view. But from your own consciousness, you always continue in a "lucky" branch. This creates the illusion of immortality, but only from the perspective of the first person. However, survival might not be pleasant. You could survive accidents, but with severe injuries, since that's still "alive."

In most universes, your body will eventually cease to function due to aging or disease. Even if you avoid accidents, your cells can't divide forever. Telomeres, the protective caps at the ends of your chromosomes, shorten, organs wear out, and so on. Therefore, in the vast majority of universes, you still die from natural causes.

However, supporters argue that there will always be some universe where a medical breakthrough, genetic quirk, or bizarre circumstance allows you to keep living. Your subjective awareness would "follow" those rare survival paths. This means you'd never experience death. Instead, you'd keep finding yourself in less and less likely branches where you continue living.

Here's the problem. The survival branches would become extremely improbable over time. You might end up existing in worlds where medicine is vastly advanced, or where you somehow don't age the same way. But that's speculation, not science. Unless aging itself is defeated in one of those universes, the body eventually fails.

Some thinkers suggest that quantum immortality could mean you continue living in very diminished states, such as extreme old age, illness, or disability. Since "being alive" includes suffering, they argue, it doesn't guarantee eternal youth, happiness, or the kind of "afterlife" many religions describe.

There's no experimental evidence that consciousness "tracks" survival across universes. There is no proof that multiple universes exist, nor any proof or evidence that this kind of afterlife is true. It is simply one of man's advanced concepts about what happens to us after we die.

To summarize, the multiverse theory, also referred to as parallel universes, posits that our universe is not the only one. There could be many universes, each with different laws of physics, constants, or histories. Its origins stem from quantum physics, specifically Hugh Everett's Many-Worlds Interpretation.

The many-worlds interpretation proposes that every possible outcome exists in its own separate universe. Cosmology suggests that during the Big Bang or the inflationary epoch, multiple bubble-like universes may have formed. These parallel universes could contain potentially infinite versions of reality.

String theory, on the other hand, is a theoretical framework in physics that attempts to explain all forces and particles as tiny, vibrating "strings" of energy, rather than point-like particles. String theory predicts ten or eleven dimensions, depending on the version. We live in four dimensions: 3D space plus time.

The others are thought to be "curled up" or hidden at scales too small for us to detect. Some physicists wonder whether these extra dimensions could harbor structures or phenomena that influence our reality but remain invisible to us.

String theory suggests that fundamental particles are tiny vibrating strings, but when combined with cosmology, it predicts the existence of a "multiverse." This multiverse isn't about branching choices like in Parallel Universes.

It involves entirely different universes with different physical laws. For example, in one universe, the gravitational force could be stronger. In another, the electron might not exist, so atoms as we know them wouldn't form. This could result in universes where life develops differently.

Some thinkers propose that consciousness might not be solely a brain process but could also involve interactions with higher dimensions. If this is true, our "soul" or "life energy," what traditions call prana, chi, or spirit, might partially exist in those extra dimensions. This could explain why consciousness feels mysterious and isn't fully explained by neurons alone.

If our "soul" is a form of energy or a pattern in higher dimensions, then when the body dies, that information might not be destroyed. It could continue in those unseen dimensions. This overlaps with ancient ideas. In Hinduism and Buddhism, prana is believed to continue in cycles, leading to reincarnation. In Christianity and Islam, the soul is believed to exist beyond the body in a separate "realm." In mysticism and New Age thought, the soul is believed to vibrate at different frequencies, much like the vibrations of a string in string theory.

Parallel Universes and String Theory. Combining these ideas provides a broader perspective. Parallel universes might each contain different "versions" of you. Extra dimensions could serve as the "bridge" where consciousness or the soul continues after death. Some even speculate that the afterlife could be just existence in another dimensional layer of reality.

Sir Roger Penrose, a Nobel Prize-winning physicist, awarded in 2020 for work on black holes, has argued that the Big Bang was not the beginning of everything, but just the start of our current cycle of the universe.

Penrose started developing his **Conformal Cyclic Cosmology (CCC)** theory in the 2000s, but the full detailed proposal was published in his 2010 book, "Cycles of Time: An Extraordinary New View of the Universe." In this book, he formally introduced the idea that our universe is just one in a series of "aeons."

Each aeon begins with a Big Bang, and it ends in an ultra-distant future when the universe has expanded so much that all matter has decayed into radiation/photons. Because photons don't experience time or scale in the usual sense, the infinite, cold, empty universe of one aeon can be mathematically reshaped into the hot, dense Big Bang of the next aeon.

Penrose suggests that traces of the previous universe might still be visible in the **Cosmic Microwave Background** (CMB), the faint radiation leftover from the Big Bang. He and his collaborators, notably Vahe Gurzadyan, reported discovering mysterious circular patterns in the CMB, sometimes referred to as "Hawking Points." They argue that this could be a signature of supermassive black holes evaporating at the end of the previous eon.

These claims are controversial, and many cosmologists argue that the patterns can be explained as statistical noise. This suggests that standard cosmology, which encompasses inflation and the Big Bang, does not require earlier universes.

Penrose believes the universe is eternal, passing through infinite cycles of birth and death. Our Big Bang wasn't the first. It was just the latest rebirth, and faint "echoes" of the prior universe that may still be imprinted in today's cosmic background radiation.

Besides string theory and parallel universes, science and fringe science explore quantum consciousness, holographic reality, simulation theory, loop quantum gravity, and panpsychism as ways to explain life, death, and awareness.

Loop Quantum Gravity, or LQG, is an alternative to string theory. Instead of tiny vibrating strings, it proposes that space-time itself is made up of discrete "chunks," similar to pixels. Some speculate that consciousness might be connected to the structure of space-time itself, not just the brain.

The **Holographic Universe Theory** suggests that the universe functions like a hologram. What we perceive as 3D reality is actually information projected from a 2D surface at the edge of the universe. If reality is fundamentally made of information, some argue that consciousness, and perhaps the soul, could also be an unbreakable pattern of information. After death, this information may not disappear, but rather change its form.

The **Simulation Hypothesis** was popularized by Nick Bostrom and is supported by Elon Musk and other prominent figures. It suggests that everything, including our universe, physical laws, and even consciousness, could be part of a highly advanced digital simulation created by an intelligent civilization, sometimes called "post-human."

Similar ideas have existed in philosophy for centuries. Plato's Allegory of the Cave and Descartes' Evil Demon thought experiment are two examples.

Plato's Allegory of the Cave appears in *The Republic, Book VII*, and was written around 380 BCE. Plato is the author using Socratic dialogue. In the story, Plato invites us to imagine a group of prisoners who have been chained deep inside a cave since birth. They face a wall and cannot turn around. Behind them burns a fire. Between the fire and the prisoners is a walkway where others carry objects, statues, and figures.

As these figures pass, their shadows are cast on the cave wall, and the prisoners, who have never seen the real objects or the outside world, believe those shadows are reality. Then, one prisoner is freed and led out of the cave. At first, he's blinded by the sunlight, since the truth is hard to face. Gradually, he sees the real objects, the sun, and realizes that the cave was an illusion. When he returns to free the others, they don't believe him. Some may even want to hurt him for challenging their beliefs.

Plato's cave is a metaphor for human perception and the pursuit of enlightenment. The shadows symbolize illusions or appearances we see with our senses. The objects stand for higher truths or eternal ideas. The sun signifies the ultimate truth or the Form of the Good. The journey out represents education, philosophy, and awakening.

"How could they see anything but the shadows if they were never allowed to move their heads?" – Plato

In modern terms, it's a warning that what we perceive could be an illusion, similar to a simulation or virtual world, and that genuine understanding requires awakening beyond surface appearances.

Descartes' evil demon, or evil genius, thought experiment first appeared in *Meditations on First Philosophy* in 1641. René Descartes is the author.

Descartes wanted to find absolute certainty. Something he could not possibly doubt, even if all his senses and reasoning deceived him. He proposed a radical form of skepticism.

"What if an all-powerful evil demon is deceiving me? Making me believe the world exists, that I have a body, that $2 + 3 = 5$? When none of it is true?"

So, he imagined a scenario in which everything he perceived was a deception created by this malicious being, a sort of ultimate illusionist. By doubting everything, including his senses and the physical world, Descartes sought something undeniable. He discovered it within his own consciousness. "I think, therefore I am." (Cogito, ergo sum.)

Even if he's being deceived, he must exist as a thinking thing to be deceived at all. So, the Evil Demon idea was a tool to strip away all uncertain beliefs, leaving only the certainty of self-awareness.

This is the philosophical ancestor of today's simulation hypothesis and brain-in-a-vat thought experiments. Replace "evil demon" with a supercomputer, and you have: "What if all your experiences are generated by code?" It forces us to ask if we can ever truly know whether the external world exists. Or are we trapped in an illusion that just feels real?

Nick Bostrom introduced the modern form in 2003. In a landmark paper, philosopher Nick Bostrom at Oxford proposed a logical trilemma in which one of these must be true:

One. Almost all civilizations go extinct before developing simulation-level computing power.

Two. Advanced civilizations lose interest in running ancestor simulations.

or

Three. We are almost certainly living in a simulation.

In other words, if one and two are false, and it's possible to create such simulations, then we're likely inside one because simulated beings would vastly outnumber "real" ones.

There are many arguments that support this idea. The first argument is the Computational Limits of Reality. Quantum mechanics suggests discrete, pixel-like units or quantized energy. Some scientists note that the universe behaves like a giant information processor.

The second argument is the Mathematical Nature of Physics. In this argument, the universe is governed by elegant mathematical laws. Like a code. Some see this as evidence of an underlying algorithmic structure.

The third argument is technological progress. In this case, we are already creating realistic simulations. Examples include VR and AI worlds. In a few centuries, a civilization could simulate entire universes.

The fourth argument supporting this theory is known as quantum weirdness. In the strange world of quantum physics, certain phenomena, such as the observer effect and quantum entanglement, don't behave according to the normal rules of classical physics. The observer effect suggests that simply observing a particle can alter its behavior, while quantum entanglement shows that two particles can remain connected and instantaneously affect each other, even when separated by vast distances.

These puzzling behaviors seem to defy logic and have led some theorists to suggest that they might be "programmatic shortcuts" within the underlying structure of reality. Almost like glitches or efficient coding tricks in a vast, simulated universe.

Of course, skeptics argue that there is a testability problem. Currently, there's no empirical way to prove or disprove the hypothesis. They point to the complexity of such a simulation. Simulating every atom in a universe is unimaginably costly. Even advanced civilizations might find it impractical.

They will also raise objections based on Anthropic bias. Just because something could be simulated doesn't mean it actually is. And, naturally, there are philosophical objections. If everything is simulated, the word "real" loses its meaning, as we would still be living a genuine existence within that framework. In this view, death might just be like logging out of the simulation, and your "true self" could exist outside of it.

To lend further credibility to this theory, John B. Calhoun conducted an experiment between 1950 and 1970 known as

"Universe 25," also referred to as the *mouse utopia experiment.* The study explored social behavior under conditions of abundance, and people have used its findings as a metaphor for human society, particularly in relation to concerns about overpopulation, urban crowding, and social collapse.

In his experiment, Calhoun created a mouse utopia. A large, enclosed environment that offered unlimited food and water, a constant comfortable temperature, no predators, ample nesting material, and complete freedom from disease and physical threats. It was designed to be an ideal environment that provided everything a mouse could need.

He started with a small number of healthy mice, usually eight individuals, and allowed them to breed freely. Calhoun observed a predictable cycle across multiple experiments. He labeled the four stages he observed as Phase A, Phase B, Phase C, and Phase D.

Phase A was also known as *the Establishment phase.* In this phase, the mice explored and formed territories. They mated and reproduced, and the population grew steadily.

During Phase B of the experiment, the utopia experienced explosive growth. With no limits, the population doubled approximately every fifty-five days. However, the mice were healthy, social, and behaved normally.

During Phase C, which Calhoun described as the *Stagnation/ Social Strain period*, density increased, and social order began to break down. Dominant males became aggressive and territorial. Subordinate males withdrew. Females became anxious and neglected their offspring, and social roles began to fragment.

During Phase D, referred to as *the Decline* or *"Behavioral Sink"* period, Birth rates collapsed. Mothers abandoned or attacked their young. Violence increased. Murder, cannibalism, and sexual deviation appeared.

Some males withdrew completely, grooming themselves excessively. Calhoun called them "the Beautiful Ones". They looked perfect but showed no interest in mating or social behavior. Eventually, the population crashes, even though all their needs were met.

By the end, despite having food, water, and safety, the colony died out completely. This suggested that social order and purpose are essential for survival and that abundance alone isn't enough.

With AI taking over our daily tasks and society depending on it for everything, we're closer than ever to seeing this experiment played out in the real world. What will we do? Will we allow humanity to fade away, or will we create simulations that give us the social order and purpose we so desperately need?

Emergent Consciousness Theories propose that consciousness naturally emerges from the inherent complexity of physical systems, much like the human brain. In this perspective, consciousness isn't a separate or mystical force. It's simply a result of matter becoming highly organized, similar to how wetness emerges when water molecules come together. This view is materialistic, meaning consciousness ceases when the brain stops functioning.

However, some thinkers take this idea a step further. If the universe itself is a vast and complex system, then perhaps consciousness isn't just limited to living brains. It could be a fundamental property of the cosmos itself. This broader view is known as panpsychism.

Panpsychism and **Integrated Information Theory** (IIT) propose that consciousness is a fundamental property of matter, similar to charge or mass. Everything possesses some level of awareness. IIT quantifies consciousness as the amount of "integrated information" within a system. These ideas suggest that "mind" isn't confined to the brain. It could be present everywhere.

No matter which of these scenarios you believe in, they all share one thing in common. The human body cannot and has not had the ability to live forever. There is a limit to how old our bodies can become. Experts have pinpointed this at around one hundred and twenty years.

Chapter Twelve

Modern science teaches that matter and energy are interchangeable. According to Einstein's famous equation, $E = mc^2$, everything that has mass, including our bodies, is actually a form of energy. This equation means that matter and energy are two sides of the same coin. Matter is simply energy in a slowed-down, structured state. Invisible energy fields hold together the atoms and particles that make up the universe, creating the solid, stable world we experience.

From a biological perspective, living beings are complex systems of organized matter powered by constant energy exchange. Our bodies are composed of cells, molecules, and atoms that continually interact with the environment through processes such as breathing, eating, moving, and thinking. Life depends on this constant flow of energy.

Scientifically speaking, we are not only energy, but rather matter structured and maintained by energy. Every heartbeat, every electrical impulse in our nervous system, and every breath we take reflects this dynamic interplay between matter and energy.

Spiritually, however, when people say, "We are energy," they often mean something deeper. They are inferring that we possess a non-material essence that transcends the physical body. This idea is connected to ancient beliefs about the soul, life force, or spirit, and the invisible energy that animates all living things and may possibly survive after death.

In modern physics, a similar perspective is also evident in **Quantum Field Theory** (QFT). According to QFT, reality is not made of solid matter, but of invisible fields of energy that fill all of space. What we think of as "particles," electrons, photons, and quarks, are actually tiny ripples or vibrations within these fields, much like waves on the surface of an ocean. In this view, what we call matter is simply energy condensed into a stable form. Our bodies, the chair you sit on, and even the air you breathe are all organized patterns of vibrating energy.

That's why so many thinkers, both scientific and spiritual, say that "everything is energy." Physics reveals that matter is composed of energy, arranged in intricate ways, while biology demonstrates that life relies on the flow of energy. When we eat, our bodies break down food into molecules that release chemical energy. Our cells use this energy to power every function of life. Within those cells, mitochondria act like miniature power plants, converting nutrients into usable energy that keeps us alive and active. Life itself, then, can be seen as a highly organized process of capturing, transforming, and releasing energy.

Some researchers have even drawn connections between this scientific understanding and ancient mysteries. For instance, the Shroud of Turin. Whether one believes the image was created at the moment of Jesus's death or at his resurrection, one theory suggests a divine burst, which could have been pure, virgin-white energy leaving or entering his body.

This burst from a pure and unadulterated soul, stained and scorched the cloth while making its way to his resurrection, and infusing our energy pool with uncorrupted goodness. This process may have offset the centuries of war and atrocities that had been inflicted on humans throughout the ages.

This same idea, that energy can leave a lasting imprint, can also be used to explain ghosts and hauntings. Cases like the Amityville house or the Einfeld poltergeist in England have been shown to be fabricated for financial gain. In each case, investigators proved that the claimants had lied, and in other instances, they were caught in the act attempting to fake the haunting.

There are other reports where people claimed spirits have harmed them, but there is no credible evidence, such as photographs or reliable witnesses, that anyone has actually been physically injured by ghosts.

Most of the ghostly sightings that left experts baffled included photos and claims of seeing a poltergeist on the stairs or wandering the grounds. If you examine these cases closely, the spirits causing the hauntings have experienced horrific deaths, torture, and atrocities so severe that the energy they carried with them could have left scars on the reality surrounding them.

Such was the case of Anne Boleyn. She was beheaded in 1535 and has been seen walking the halls with her severed head in her hands. On the Myrtles Plantation in Louisiana, Chloe, the slave, is seen wandering the grounds. The one common denominator in all of the unexplained hauntings is the horrors and violent, unjustified deaths they endured.

These unimaginable horrors could cause energy to distort, warping the fabric of space-time and leaving an image on the fabric of our reality. Almost like a photo or short movie, they play on the surroundings where the atrocities occurred.

Yet, while this unexplained phenomenon still baffles investigators, others believe that intense emotional events such as tragedy, love, fear, or violence can leave behind energetic "imprints" in the environment.

If our energy is powerful enough to scorch a shroud or leave a lasting impression on reality, couldn't it also be passed on through reincarnation, enter a pleasure palace, or drift into a gray void of nothingness?

This is where physics intersects with philosophy. In mainstream physics, consciousness is not defined as "energy." It remains an open question in neuroscience and philosophy.

Roger Penrose and anesthesiologist Stuart Hameroff proposed **quantum consciousness** (Orch-OR theory) in the 1990s. It suggests consciousness arises from quantum processes within neurons located inside microtubules. If consciousness is a quantum phenomenon, it might not be strictly limited to the brain, and could, in theory, continue in some form after biological death. Some argue that consciousness might be linked to quantum processes in the brain.

Hameroff proposed that microtubules process information at a deeper level than just neuron-to-neuron firing. Penrose argued that the brain might use quantum mechanics, the physics of subatomic particles, for thinking. Normally, quantum states collapse randomly. However, Penrose suggested an objective rule, which he termed Objective Reduction, that determines when and how they collapse.

If quantum collapses occur in microtubules and are "orchestrated" by the brain's biology, this could generate moments of conscious awareness. So, consciousness is not merely computation. It's connected to fundamental physics. It links physics, biology, and the mind together.

If this idea is correct, then consciousness could be linked to the very foundation of the universe itself, not merely a byproduct of brain chemistry. It could explain mysterious experiences such as near-death visions, intuition, or why anesthesia can instantly switch consciousness off by disrupting quantum processes in the brain.

Skeptics, however, remain doubtful. Most neuroscientists argue that quantum effects can't survive in the brain's warm, biological environment. They believe consciousness arises from complex networks of neurons, rather than from quantum physics.

Others say there's no solid experimental evidence yet. And still others believe Penrose's "objective reduction" isn't well-defined. Others suggest consciousness could be a kind of emergent "energy pattern" in the brain, not reducible to just matter.

Ultimately, physics reveals that matter is composed of organized energy, and biology demonstrates that life depends on the flow of energy. Some modern theories even propose that consciousness itself might be part of this vast, interconnected energetic web.

So while saying "we are nothing but energy" oversimplifies things, it's fair to say that we are systems of matter, energy, and information woven together in intricate balance, part of a living universe that continuously transforms energy into form and back again.

Let's explore how major scientific and philosophical thinkers have described life and consciousness in terms of energy.

Albert Einstein lived from 1879 to 1955. He was one of the most renowned and influential scientists of all time. Best known for his theory of relativity and the iconic equation $E = mc^2$, he demonstrated that matter and energy are interchangeable, forever transforming our understanding of the universe.

He once explained, "Energy cannot be created or destroyed. It can only be changed from one form to another." While Einstein never claimed that consciousness itself was energy, his discoveries laid the foundation for the modern view that everything physical, including living beings, is ultimately an expression of energy.

On a more philosophical note, Einstein often spoke of what he called a "cosmic religious feeling," meaning he felt that humanity is deeply connected to a vast, mysterious, and orderly universe. Many interpret this as being in harmony with the idea that existence is fundamentally energetic and interconnected.

Erwin Schrödinger was an Austrian physicist who received the Nobel Prize in Physics and lived from 1887 to 1961. He is considered one of the pioneers of quantum mechanics and authored the book

'What is Life?' in 1944. He described life as "negative entropy" or "negentropy."

He believed living beings maintain order by constantly importing energy and expelling disorder into the environment. Schrödinger leaned toward a non-dual philosophy, influenced by Vedanta. He suggested that at the deepest level, there is only one universal consciousness, and that individual minds are like waves on that ocean.

Advaita Vedānta is one of the major schools of Hindu philosophy. Its core teaching is that Ātman, which is the true self or soul, and Brahman, the ultimate reality or Absolute, are one and the same. The apparent separateness of individuals, the world, and God is referred to as Māyā, meaning illusion or misperception. Liberation (moksha) is achieved by realizing this non-dual truth, often through self-inquiry, meditation, and scriptural study.

Niels Bohr, another quantum pioneer, introduced the idea of complementarity. He lived from 1885 to 1962. In complementarity, light, along with other quantum entities, can act like a particle in some experiments but more like a wave that spreads out or ripples energy in others. Both descriptions are accurate, but you can't observe both aspects simultaneously. They are complementary views of the same reality.

Some thinkers drew inspiration from physics and applied this concept to consciousness and matter. Instead of viewing the mind and matter as completely separate (dualism), or claiming that one can be reduced to the other (materialism or idealism), they suggest that both are complementary aspects of a single, deeper reality.

Just like light can be a wave or particle depending on how you observe it, reality can be experienced as matter from an external perspective in physics or biology, or as consciousness from an internal, first-person perspective.

Bohr himself avoided speculating about consciousness, but his physics suggested that the act of observation (mind) and energy (matter) are closely connected.

Max Planck, who lived from 1858 to 1947, was the founder of Quantum Theory. He is well known for saying, "I regard consciousness as fundamental. I regard matter as derivative from consciousness. We cannot get behind consciousness." This is one of the strongest statements from a physicist suggesting that the mind, not matter, might be primary, and that energy or matter could arise from consciousness itself.

Roger Penrose is a modern-day theorist born in 1931. Penrose believes that consciousness is not merely computation, like a machine, but is rooted in quantum processes within the brain. Alongside anesthesiologist Stuart Hameroff, he developed the Orch-OR theory (Orchestrated Objective Reduction) in the 1990s.

There are other perspectives. For example, **Teilhard de Chardin**, who lived from 1881 to 1955, was a philosopher and Jesuit priest. He viewed evolution as progressing toward an "Omega Point" where consciousness and energy merge into a cosmic unity.

Today, most scientists still see consciousness as an emergent property of the brain's energy use. A product of neurons firing in astonishing harmony. Yet others continue to ask whether, at the deepest level, we and the universe are one vast field of energy and awareness, experiencing itself through countless forms of life.

Chapter Thirteen

For as long as humans have walked the earth, we've gazed upward at the stars, downward into the soil, and inward into our own hearts. We've wondered what happened to our friends and family when that spark, that glow, that inner life has left, and their eyes are left blank and unmoving.

We've also wondered with fear about what will happen when we die. What becomes of the essence that animates us, the awareness that smiles, weeps, loves, and dreams, and the knowledge and experiences that we have accumulated through our years of existence?

We know what happens physically. The body, once animated, begins its gradual return to the earth. Cells break down, energy disperses, the heartbeat stills, and the life force exits the body. But what of the non-physical? What of the part of us that observes, feels, and knows? Does it simply flicker out, like a candle in the wind, or does it transform into something else? Something unseen, but eternal?

We've examined religious beliefs about death and dying, traced creation stories across continents, explored near-death experiences, and reviewed reincarnation cases that challenge conventional explanations. We've examined ancient texts that suggest the body is not what truly evolves. It's the spirit or conscious energy within.

This chapter is not meant to preach one truth over another. Instead, it is an exploration. A walk through science, spirituality, and philosophy to see whether perhaps, in the tapestry of all beliefs, there is a single thread of unity. After all, even the greatest myth may hold a kernel of truth, and even the most elegant theory may still glimpse only a shadow of reality.

Across cultures and eras, human beings have told stories to make sense of life and death. From the ancient Egyptians preparing for the afterlife with elaborate tombs, to the Tibetan Book of the Dead describing consciousness crossing into new forms, to the Aboriginal Dreamtime, where spirits return to the ancestral plane. The theme repeats. Life is a journey of separation and return.

Even today, modern science grapples with questions once reserved for mystics. Are there parallel universes? Could consciousness be fundamental, and woven into the fabric of the cosmos itself? Might death simply be a transition, a shift from one state to another?

We've explored string theory, which suggests multiple dimensions vibrating beyond perception. We've examined quantum mechanics, which challenges our understanding of observation and reality. And we've listened to near-death experiences, where countless people describe leaving their bodies, traveling through light, and encountering overwhelming love. These experiences defy traditional explanation yet echo across cultures.

Modern science has given us astonishing tools to understand the visible world. We've explored parallel universes, string theory, and quantum realities. We've found hints that reality is deeper and stranger than what meets the eye. Yet, even as we uncover new dimensions, the question remains. Which of these views is correct?

What if they are all correct, in their own way? And it's up to each of us to perceive the truth they point toward? What if, rather than choosing one version, we allow all truths to coexist, each reflecting part of the same infinite whole? Perhaps reality is a prism, each tradition reflecting one facet of the same light.

Before diving into the metaphysical, we must begin with what we know. Energy is what sustains human life. From a purely scientific perspective, energy is the foundation of all life. Complex forms of energy moving through and around us power every heartbeat, every breath, every thought.

All living beings are engines of energy transformation. From the moment we take our first breath, our cells engage in an endless dance of creation and renewal. In physics, energy is never created nor destroyed. It's only transformed. The energy of our bodies comes from sunlight captured by plants, from the food we consume, and from the oxygen we breathe. Life itself is an exquisite chain of energy transfer.

In biological terms, our power stems from the chemical energy stored in a molecule called ATP (adenosine triphosphate). ATP is the "currency" of life. A rechargeable battery that stores energy within its high-energy phosphate bonds. Every heartbeat, every muscle contraction, every neuron firing in the brain, draws upon the high-energy bonds of ATP. Without it, life ceases instantly.

Our electrical energy flows through the nervous system. Tiny surges of current leaping across synapses, forming the foundation of thought, motion, and memory. Our thermal energy radiates as body heat. The glow of metabolism that keeps us warm and alive. Our kinetic energy is expressed in the motion of the graceful arc of a dancer's arm, the pulse of blood through veins, and the rhythm of breathing.

All these energies obey the laws of physics. They are measurable, quantifiable, and bound by Einstein's theory of relativity. The speed of light is the cosmic speed limit, and the fastest that anything in the universe can travel. When we die, these energies do not vanish. They transform, dispersing into the environment, rejoining the greater web of matter and energy.

But what about the part of us that thinks, feels, loves, and dreams? What about the sense of "I am?" That I exist. What about consciousness, the spark behind the eyes? Science has yet to pin down its source or boundaries. That is where physics ends, and philosophy and metaphysics begin.

We can map the brain, measure neurons, and track impulses, but awareness itself, the experiencer behind the eyes, remains a mystery. Is it a byproduct of matter? Or is matter a vessel for something greater? This question bridges science and spirituality. Many traditions claim that what we truly are is not the body, but the life source. A conscious energy that preexists and outlives the flesh.

From a metaphysical perspective, our life source, often referred to as the soul, spirit, or conscious energy, transcends what can be measured. It is not bound by the speed of light or spatial dimensions. Upon death, this essence is released, carrying within it the knowledge, memories, and experiences of a lifetime.

Its speed, if it can be called that, is instantaneous. Upon death, this essence is released, carrying the imprint of our life. All our memories, emotions, intentions, and lessons are contained within our essence. Like a traveler shedding a worn-out cloak, the soul steps beyond physical limitations and rejoins the unseen realm.

According to Stephen Hawking, energy can be swallowed by black holes. It was originally thought that this would destroy the information it carried, but he revised his theory to say that black holes can "spit" energy back into the universe. He called this discharge "Hawking radiation" and theorized that it does not destroy information but rather transforms it.

The story of the Egyptian god Anubis weighing the heart to Ma'at's feather, and having Ammit eat it if it was heavier than the feather, as well as the Polynesian beliefs of Máori Whiro, who fed on bodies to gain power, could be a crude reference to black holes and how a life could truly die, transform or be delayed to its destination for eons. It could be a warning to wandering souls not ready to give up this realm.

However, if consciousness is indeed energy, and we know that energy will persist. The question is, where does it go? We know it cannot simply vanish. It must reach its like energy and transform.

It's difficult to imagine a soul wandering endlessly through a silent void or being trapped in a gravitational well like a black hole for all eternity, but these images stir the imagination and hint at how consciousness might transcend the physical.

The creation stories of the world offer clues. Again and again, we see the same pattern. A beginning, a journey, and a return. Some describe a gray, shadowy realm. Others describe a radiant paradise, and still others describe it as a place of purification or sorrow.

Across myths and sciences alike, a recurring image appears. A pool, a sea, a field. The Greeks called it the "aether." Quantum physicists refer to it as the field or quantum vacuum. An ocean of potential from which particles arise. Mystics refer to it as the Source, Spirit, or God.

Physics tells us that like energy attracts like energy. Across all existence, from atoms to galaxies, patterns emerge through attraction and resonance. Every living and non-living thing. Every star, tree, and heartbeat is part of this universal energy field.

Perhaps at death, our conscious essence, the totality of our being , dissolves back into the pool. Some return swiftly, merging seamlessly with the whole. Others, reluctant or unready, may linger in turbulence, clinging to identity, to ego, to unfinished stories. These experiences could be what some call purgatory, limbo, or the shadow realms. They could also be the same souls that could wander into black holes. This idea echoes the teachings of many faiths.

Some envision a heaven, others a reincarnation, others a state of pure awareness. The ancient Egyptians spoke of crossing the Duat, the Tibetans of traversing the Bardo, the Christians of ascending to the Father's house, the Hindus of merging into Brahman. They all had different paths, yet the same horizon. They all return home.

Like energy attracts like energy. The pool organizes itself through resonance. Kindness calls to kindness. Hatred attracts hatred. Those who release easily, surrendering the ego, dissolve peacefully. Those who cling to self, to anger, to fear, may find themselves in a dim or turbulent realm, a "gray place" reflecting their struggle. In this way, our inner state determines our experience in the afterlife. Not as punishment or reward, but as alignment.

Imagine standing at the edge of a vast ocean, holding a single drop of water on the tip of your finger. When you release it, the drop meets the sea, and it sends out a ripple. A brief signature of its arrival. Then, in an instant, it's absorbed, its molecules mingling with countless others. The individual drop disappears, yet every molecule remains, but now it's part of the infinite sea. No boundary separates it from the whole as it becomes part of something vast and eternal.

So it may be with us. Throughout our lives, we perceive ourselves as separate individuals with names, histories, and dreams. We are never truly separate from the ocean. Our individuality is a temporary illusion. At death, the illusion dissolves, and we rejoin the whole.

In truth, we have always been the ocean, experiencing itself through a single drop. Spiritually, this symbolizes our journey. From the perspective of eternity, the process is instantaneous. A blink in cosmic time.

When a new soul is born, it may draw from this energy pool, gathering fragments of prior experience, bits of memory, talents, and inclinations. This could be why the religions of the day say we are made in the image of God.

It's because a small piece of God, Jesus, Shakespeare, Beethoven, and even Hitler resides inside of us all. We have all past lives, all past experiences, all past emotions and feelings that artists, prophets, killers, royals, and commoners have experienced. The divine image, as religions say, may not be a face but a composition. A reflection of all that has ever been.

When the extraction of a new soul occurs, it's possible that those who clung to the self, the fear, the anger, the shock, or a violent death could remain with their like energy within the pool. This could explain the reports of unexplained reincarnation.

It could also explain a child composing symphonies or painting masterpieces beyond their years. Could the like energy of music or of art have gathered together within the concept of like energy attracting like energy?

Could we all be recalling other lives? Could we all be accessing residual fragments within their energy field? Could more of the evil experiences possess the mind of some more than others? Could those tendencies be brought from our own pool of existence?

If so, our essence contains multitudes. We hold the potential for greatness and cruelty, wisdom and folly. But potential is not destiny. We are not puppets of our composition. We are creators, shaping meaning through our choices.

Just as a soul blessed with the molecules of a musician may never play an instrument, a person gifted with brilliance may waste it. Likewise, one who inherits darker impulses can transcend them through love, service, and awareness. The energy we are given is clay. Our choices are the sculptor's hands.

This is the essence of free will. We are co-authors of creation. With every thought, word, and deed, we feed certain patterns, strengthening kindness or cruelty, humility or pride. These energies ripple outward, not only shaping our destiny but influencing the entire pool.

In this light, morality is not about fear of punishment or promise of reward, but about vibration. Each act adds its tone to the universal chord. Over lifetimes, we tune ourselves toward harmony or dissonance, unity or chaos.

Since the dawn of time, humanity has told stories of good and evil, light and darkness. From Adam and Eve's temptation to modern tales of heroes conquering shadows, the struggle has been our oldest companion. Yet the battlefield is not "out there," it is within.

Each thought, word, and deed we contribute ripples into the cosmic pool. Our positivity and negativity, our love and hatred, merge with the whole. Over lifetimes, we shape the balance of our being, edging toward light or darkness.

If all existence is evolving, not merely biologically but spiritually, then every choice feeds into what we, and the universe, become. There cannot be good without evil, joy without sorrow, hunger without fullness. Duality defines experience. But balance defines growth.

Just as there have been righteous deities and evil deities in Greek and Roman mythology, there must be good and evil in the world we are about to enter. Our next evolution. Not as one but as a whole. When we reach the culmination of our journey. When our essence tips wholly toward one side or the other, that is the entity we shall become. In the grand pattern of creation, both light and shadow are necessary threads. And it is our choice as a people, as a society, as a group, as a whole to decide what it is we will evolve into.

And so we turn to one of the wisest stories ever told. *The Tale of the Two Wolves.*

An old Cherokee elder once told his grandson:

"A fight is going on inside me. It is a terrible fight, and it is between two wolves.

One is evil: anger, envy, greed, arrogance, resentment, lies, and ego.

The other is good — joy, peace, love, hope, humility, kindness, truth, and compassion.

The same fight is going on inside you — and inside every other person, too."

The boy thought for a moment, then asked.

"Grandfather, which wolf will win?"

The elder smiled.

"The one you feed."

This simple wisdom distills all philosophy, religion, and psychology into one truth. We become what we nurture. The soul we build is the soul that returns to the pool. By feeding love rather than hatred, gratitude rather than envy, and compassion rather than cruelty, we elevate not only ourselves but the entire web of existence.

Perhaps we return home. To the pool. The source. The ocean of consciousness from which all life springs. There, our experiences become part of the collective symphony, influencing the next wave of creation. Our task is not to escape this cycle, but to shape it. To feed the right wolf. To contribute love, wisdom, and beauty to the current that carries us all.

Every act of kindness, every spark of creativity, every whisper of forgiveness adds light to the pool. Conversely, every act of violence and war, every statement or feeling of hate, anger, and jealousy, every whisper of evil adds darkness to not only the pool but to all of us.

In the end, we are not a drop in the ocean. We are the entire ocean in a drop. How we choose our evolution to mature is our choice. How we allow our society to exist is our responsibility. What will you choose?

.

www.ingramcontent.com/pod-product-compliance
Lightning Source LLC
Chambersburg PA
CBHW020911090426
42736CB00008B/588